THE NON-DESIGNER'S DESIGN BOOK

THE Non- Designer's Design Book

design

and

typographic

principles

for the

visual

novice

Robin Williams

Peachpit Press
Berkeley
California

◪ The Non-Designer's Design Book

R O B I N   W I L L I A M S

Peachpit Press
2414 Sixth Street
Berkeley, CA 94710
510/548-4393
510/548-5991 (fax)

Peachpit Press is a division of Addison-Wesley Publishing Company.

Copyright © 1994 by Robin Williams

Copyeditor: Carole Quandt
Cover design: Robin Williams
Interior design: Robin Williams
Production: Robin Williams

The quote by Jan White on page 117 is from the wonderful book How to Spec Type, by Alex White. Reprinted courtesy of Roundtable Press, Inc. Copyright 1987 by Roundtable Press, Inc.

The delightful pen-and-ink drawing of the wicket woof on pages 38 and 39 are by Jon Vlakos, reprinted courtesy of Swamp Press. Copyright 1990 by Swamp Press. You can order an exquisite little handmade letterpressed booklet of the tale of "Ladle Rat Rotten Hut," by Howard L. Chace. Send $2 per booklet, plus $1.75 per order to Swamp Press, 323 Pelham Road, Amherst, MA, 01002.

The portions of other stories, such as "Guilty Looks Enter Tree Beers," "Center Alley," and "Violate Huskings" are from a long out-of-print book by Howard L. Chace called Anguish Languish. It is our understanding that these stories are now in the public domain. However, we have had great difficulty in obtaining positive proof of this. We would be ever so grateful if someone could provide us with any more information so we could truly give due credit and help to further promote Mr. Chace's concept of the Anguish Languish. These stories are so delightful that we wanted to share them with the world.

Notice of Liability
The information in this book is distributed on an "As Is" basis, without warranty. While every precaution has been taken in the preparation of the book, neither the author nor Peachpit Press shall have any liability to any person or entity with respect to any loss or damage caused or alleged to be caused directly or indirectly by the instructions contained in this book or by the computer software and hardware products described in it.

ISBN 1-56609-159-4

Tenth Printing

To Carmen Karr,
my comrade in Design,
my friend in Life.
— with great love,
R.

More matter is being printed and published today than ever before, and every publisher of an advertisement, pamphlet, or book expects his material to be read. Publishers and, even more so, readers want what is important to be clearly laid out. They will not read anything that is troublesome to read, but are pleased with what looks clear and well arranged, for it will make their task of understanding easier. For this reason, the important part must stand out and the unimportant must be subdued . . . .

The technique of modern typography must also adapt itself to the speed of our times. Today, we cannot spend as much time on a letter heading or other piece of jobbing as was possible even in the nineties.

—Jan Tschichold, 1955

Contents

Design principles

1 **The Joshua Tree Principle   13**

    Proximity
    Alignment
    Repetition
    Contrast

2 **Proximity   15**

    The basic purpose
    How to get it
    What to avoid

3 **Alignment   27**

    The basic purpose
    How to get it
    What to avoid

4 **Repetition   43**

    The basic purpose
    How to get it
    What to avoid

5 **Contrast   53**

    The basic purpose
    How to get it
    What to avoid

Designing with type

Extras

But, is it appropriate?
—*Edward Gottschall*

It stinks.
—*Herb Lubalin*

Is this book for you?

This book is written for all the people who now need to design pages, but have no background or formal training in design. I don't mean just those who are designing fancy packaging or lengthy brochures—I mean the secretaries whose bosses now tell them to design the newsletters, the church volunteers who are putting out information to their congregations, the small business owners who are creating their own advertising, the students who understand that a better-looking paper often means a better grade, the professionals who realize that an attractive presentation garners greater respect, the teachers who have learned that students respond more positively to information that is well laid out, the statisticians who are seeing that numbers and stats can be arranged in a way that invites reading rather than sleeping, and on and on.

This book assumes you don't have the time or the interest to study design and typography, but you *would* like to know how to make your pages look better. Well, the premise of this book is age-old: *knowledge is power.* Most people can look at a poorly designed page and state that they don't like it, *but they don't know what to do to fix it.* In this book I will point out four basic concepts that are used in virtually every well-designed job. These concepts are clear and concrete. If you don't know what's wrong with it, how can you fix it? Once you recognize the concepts, you will notice whether or not they have been applied to your pages. *Once you can name the problem, you can find the solution.*

This book is not intended to take the place of four years of design school. I do not pretend that you will automatically become a brilliant designer after you read and apply this little book. But I do guarantee that you will never again look at a page in the same way. I guarantee if you follow these basic principles, your work will look more professional, organized, unified, and interesting. And *you* will feel empowered.

With a smile,

Robin

Mini-glossary

The following are terms used in this book. For a complete glossary of design and typographic terms, see another book of mine, *How to Boss Your Fonts Around.*

The **baseline** is the invisible line that type sits on (see page 94).

Body copy, body text, and sometimes just plain **body** or **text** refer to the main block of text that you read, as opposed to head-lines, subheads, titles, etc. Body text is usually between 9 and 12 point type.

A **bullet** is a little marker, typically used in a list instead of numbers, or between words. This is the standard bullet: • .

A **dingbat** is a small, ornamental character, like this: ■❖✓✍ ❤. You might have the fonts Zapf Dingbats or WingDings, which are made up of dingbats.

Elements are the separate objects on the page. An element might be a single line of text, or a graphic, or a group of items that are so close together they are perceived as one unit. To know the number of elements on a page, squint your eyes and count the number of times your eye stops, seeing each separate item.

Extended text refers to the body copy (as above) when there is a lot of it, as in a book or a long report.

When I talk of your **eye** or the **eye flow,** I am referring to your eyes as if they are one independent body. You can control the way someone moves their eyes around a page (the eye flow), so you need to become more conscious of how *your* eye moves around on the page.

Justified type is when a block of text is lined up on both the left and right edges.

A **rule** is a line, a drawn line, such as the one under the headline "Mini-glossary."

White space is the space on a page that is not occupied by any text or graphics. You might call it "blank" space. Beginners tend to be afraid of white space; professional designers "use" lots of white space.

Trapped white space is when the white, or blank, space on a page is trapped between elements (such as text or photos), with no space through which to flow.

The Joshua Tree Principle

This short chapter explains the four basic principles in general, each of which will be explained in detail in the following chapters. But first I want to tell you a little story that made me realize the importance of being able to name things, since naming these principles is the key to power over them.

Many years ago I received a tree identification book for Christmas. I was at my parents' home, and after all the gifts had been opened I decided to go out and identify the trees in the neighborhood. Before I went out, I read through part of the book. The first tree in the book was the Joshua tree because it only took two clues to identify it. Now the Joshua tree is a really weird-looking tree and I looked at that picture and said to myself, "Oh, we don't have that kind of tree in Northern California. That is a weird-looking tree. I would know if I saw that tree, and I've never seen one before." So I took my book and went outside. My parents lived in a cul-de-sac of six homes. Four of those homes had Joshua trees in the front yard. I had lived in that house for thirteen years, and I had never seen a Joshua tree. I took a walk around the block, and there must have been a sale at the nursery when everyone was landscaping their new homes—at least 80 percent of the homes had Joshua trees in the front yards. *And I had never seen one before!* Once I was conscious of the tree, once I could name it, I saw it everywhere. Which is exactly my point. Once you can name something, you're conscious of it. You have power over it. You own it. You're in control.

So now you're going to learn the names of several design principles. And you are going to be in control of your pages.

The four basic principles

The following is a brief overview of the principles. Although I discuss each of these separately, keep in mind they are really interconnected. Rarely will you apply only one principle.

Contrast

The idea behind contrast is to avoid elements on the page that are merely *similar*. If the elements (type, color, size, line thickness, shape, space, etc.) are not the *same*, then make them **very different.** Contrast is often the most important visual attraction on a page.

Repetition

Repeat visual elements of the design throughout the piece. You can repeat color, shape, texture, spatial relationships, line thicknesses, sizes, etc. This helps develop the organization and strengthens the unity.

Alignment

Nothing should be placed on the page arbitrarily. Every element should have some visual connection with another element on the page. This creates a clean, sophisticated, fresh look.

Proximity

Items relating to each other should be grouped close together. When several items are in close proximity to each other, they become one visual unit rather than several separate units. This helps organize information and reduces clutter.

Umm . . .

When culling these principles from the vast morass of design theory, I thought there must be some appropriate and memorable acronym within these conceptual ideas that would help people remember them. Well, uh, there is a memorable—but very inappropriate—acronym. Sorry.

Proximity

Very often in beginners' designs, the words and phrases and graphics are strung out all over the place, filling corners and taking up lots of room so there won't be any empty space. There seems to be a fear of empty space. When pieces of a design are scattered all over, the page appears unorganized and the information may not be instantly accessible to the reader.

The principle of proximity states that you **group related items together,** move them physically close to each other, so the related items are seen as one cohesive group rather than a bunch of unrelated bits. Items or groups of information that are *not* related to each other should *not* be in close proximity (nearness) to the other elements, which gives the reader an instant visual clue as to the organization and content of the page. The following pages illustrate this principle.

Take a look at this typical business card, below. How many separate elements do you see in that small space? How many times does your eye stop to look at something?

▼ Does your eye stop five times? Of course—there are five separate items on this little card. Where do you begin reading? In the middle, probably, because that phrase is boldest. What do you read next—left to right (because you read English)? What happens when you get to the bottom right corner, where does your eye go? Does it wander around making sure you didn't miss any corners?

Reilly Pickett   (717) 555-1212

Toad Hall

916 Old River Road   Red River, NM

▼ And what if I confuse the issue even further:

Reilly Pickett   (717) 555-1212

Toad Hall

916 Old River Road   Red River, NM

▲ Now that there are two bold phrases, where do you begin? Do you start in the upper left? Do you start in the center? After you read those two items, where do you go? Perhaps you bounce back and forth between the bold words, nervously trying to catch the other words in the corners. Do you know when you're finished? Does your friend follow the same pattern you did? No?

When several items are in close proximity to each other, they become *one* visual unit rather than several *separate* units. As in life, **the proximity, or the closeness, implies a relationship.**

By grouping similar elements into one unit, several things instantly happen. The page becomes more organized. You understand where to begin reading the message, and you know when you are finished. And the "white space" (the space around the letters) becomes more organized as well.

▼ A problem with the previous card is that not one of the items on the card seems related to any other item. It is not clear where you should begin reading the card, and it is not clear when you are finished.

If I do *one thing* to this business card— if I group related elements together, into closer proximity—look what happens:

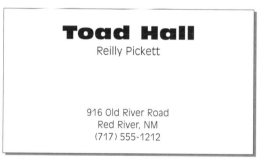

Toad Hall
Reilly Pickett

916 Old River Road
Red River, NM
(717) 555-1212

▲ Is there any question now about where you begin to read the card? About where you end? Do you know when you've gotten to the end? With that one simple concept, this card is now organized both intellectually and visually.

Shown below is a typical newsletter masthead. How many separate elements are in this piece? Does any item of information seem related to any other, judging from their placement?

▼ Take a moment to decide which items should be grouped into closer proximity, and which should be separated.

▲ The two items on the top left are in close proximity to each other, implying a relationship. Should these two **have** a relationship?

▼ Was this your logical conclusion? Have the proper relationships been established?

▲ Notice I did a couple of other things along the way:

Changed everything from all caps to lowercase, which gave me room to make the title strong and bold, and which made the text easier to read.

Changed the corners from rounded to straight, giving it a cleaner, stronger look.

Enlarged the trees and let them break out of the boundary, a common graphic trick.

When you create a flyer, a brochure, a newsletter, or whatever, you *know* which pieces of information are logically connected, you know which information should be emphasized, and what can be de-emphasized. Express that information graphically by grouping it.

CD ROMs
CD ROMs
Children's CDs
Educational CDs
Entertainment CDs
Laser discs
Educational
Early learning
Language arts
Science
Math
Teacher Tools
Books
Teacher tools
Videos
Hardware &
Accessories
Cables
Input devices
Mass storage
Memory
Modems
Printers & supplies
Video and sound

CD ROMs
CD ROMs
Children's CDs
Educational CDs
Entertainment CDs
Laser discs

Educational
Early learning
Language arts
Science
Math

Teacher Tools
Books
Teacher tools
Videos

Hardware & Accessories
Cables
Input devices
Mass storage
Memory
Modems
Printers & supplies
Video and sound

▲ Obviously, this list needs some formatting to make it understandable. But the biggest problem with this list is that everything is close to everything else, so there is no way to see the relationships or the organization.

▲ This same list has been formed into visual groups. I'm sure you already do this automatically—I'm just suggesting that you now do it **consciously** and with more strength.

Notice I added some contrast to the headlines, and repeated that contrast and the rule (line).

Sometimes when grouping like items in close proximity, you need to make some changes, such as in the size or weight or placement of text or graphics. Text does not have to be 12 point! Information that is subsidiary to the main message, such as the volume number and year of the newsletter, can often be as small as 7 or 8 point.

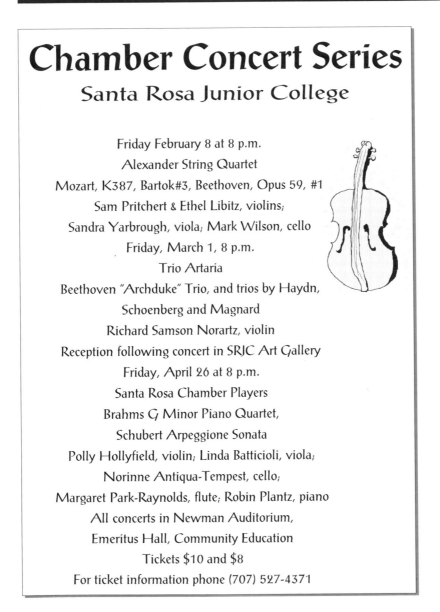

Chamber Concert Series
Santa Rosa Junior College

Friday February 8 at 8 p.m.

Alexander String Quartet

Mozart, K387, Bartok#3, Beethoven, Opus 59, #1

Sam Pritchert & Ethel Libitz, violins;

Sandra Yarbrough, viola; Mark Wilson, cello

Friday, March 1, 8 p.m.

Trio Artaria

Beethoven "Archduke" Trio, and trios by Haydn,

Schoenberg and Magnard

Richard Samson Norartz, violin

Reception following concert in SRJC Art Gallery

Friday, April 26 at 8 p.m.

Santa Rosa Chamber Players

Brahms G Minor Piano Quartet,

Schubert Arpeggione Sonata

Polly Hollyfield, violin; Linda Batticioli, viola;

Norinne Antiqua-Tempest, cello;

Margaret Park-Raynolds, flute; Robin Plantz, piano

All concerts in Newman Auditorium,

Emeritus Hall, Community Education

Tickets $10 and $8

For ticket information phone (707) 527-4371

▲ Not only is this page visually boring, but it is difficult to find the information—exactly what is going on, where is it happening, what time is it at, etc.

The idea of proximity doesn't mean that *everything* is closer together; it means elements that are *intellectually* connected, that have some sort of communication relationship, should also be *visually* connected. Other separate elements or groups of elements should *not* be in close proximity. The closeness *or* lack of closeness indicates the relationship.

Chamber Concert Series

Alexander String Quartet
Mozart, K387, Bartok#3, Beethoven, Opus 59 #1
Sam Pritchert & Ethel Libitz, violins;
Sandra Yarbrough, viola; Mark Wilson, cello
Friday, February 8, 8 P.M.

Trio Artaria
Beethoven "Archduke" Trio,
and trios by Haydn, Schoenberg and Magnard
Richard Samson Norartz, violin
Friday, March 1, 8 P.M.
Reception following concert in SRJC Art Gallery

Santa Rosa Chamber Players
Brahms G Minor Piano Quartet, Schubert Arpeggione Sonata
Polly Hollyfield, violin; Linda Batticioli, viola;
Norinne Antiqua-Tempest, cello;
Margaret Park-Raynolds, flute; Robin Plantz, piano
Friday, April 26, 8 P.M.

All concerts in Newman Auditorium, Emeritus Hall
Santa Rosa Junior College
Community Education
Tickets $10 and $8
For ticket information phone **527.4371**

▲ The information was first intellectually grouped together (in my head or sketched onto paper), then physically set in groups on the page. Notice the spacing between the three performances is the same, indicating that these three groups are somehow related. The subsidiary information is farther away—you instantly know it is not one of the performances.

You are probably already using the principle of proximity in your work, but you may not be pushing it as far as you could to make it truly effective. Really look at those pages, at those elements, and see which items should be grouped together.

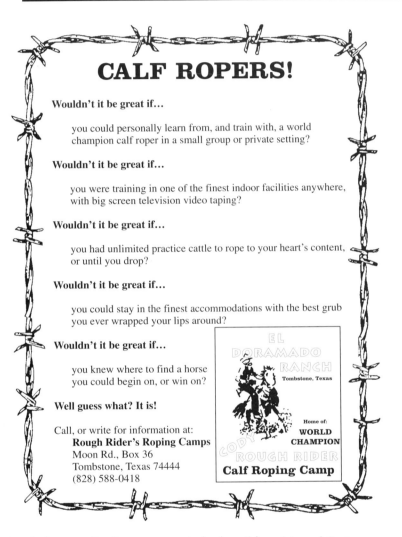

▲ Apparently the person designing this ad typed two Returns after each headline and paragraph of body copy. Thus the headlines are each the same distance from the body copy above and below, so they appear to be separate, unconnected items.

There is lots of white space available here, but it is all broken up. And there is white space where it doesn't belong, like between the headline and its related body copy. When white space is "trapped" like this, it tends to visually push the elements apart.

If there are too many separate items, see which ones should be set closer to each other. If there are areas on the page where the organization is not perfectly clear, see if items are in proximity that *shouldn't* be.

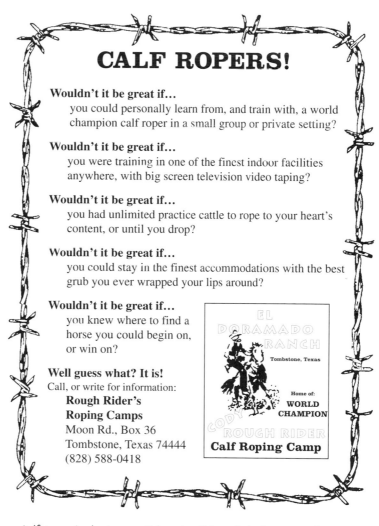

▲ If we do just one thing to this ad, just move the headlines closer to their related paragraphs of text, several things happen:

The organization is clearer. The white space is not trapped within elements. The type could be one point size larger (up to 9 point), making it easier to read the main text. There is more room so the mini-poster is not so crowded.

Proximity is really just a matter of being a little more conscious, of doing what you do naturally, but pushing the concept a little further. Once you become aware of the importance of the relationships between lines of type, you will start noticing its effect. Once you start noticing the effect, you own it, you have power over it, you are in control.

▲ I took this ad right out of the newspaper. Really. One of the biggest problems with it (besides being all caps) is that all the information is one big hunk.

Before trying to design with this information, write out the separate pieces of information that belong together; group the elements. You know how to do this—simply use your brain.

Once you have the groups of information, you can play with them on the page.

Rarely is applying the principle of proximity the only answer to a problematic page. The other three principles are intrinsic to the design process and you will usually find yourself using all four. Take them one at a time—*start* with proximity.

▲ This is only one of a buzzillion possibilities for arranging the groups of information. I also used the principles of alignment and contrast, which you will be reading about shortly.

But the biggest problem with the original ad is that there is no separation of information. All the text in all caps in one big block also took up all the space, so there was no extra, blank, "white" space to rest your eyes. It's okay to set the type smaller than 12 or 14 point! Really!

Summary of Proximity

When several items are in close proximity to each other, they become one visual unit rather than several separate units. Items relating to each other should be grouped together. Be conscious of where your eye is going: where do you start looking; what path do you follow; where do you end up; after you've read it, where does your eye go next? You should be able to follow a logical progression through the piece, from a definite beginning to a definite end.

The basic purpose

The basic purpose of proximity is to organize. Other principles come into play as well, but simply grouping related elements together into closer proximity automatically creates organization. If the information is organized, it is more likely to be read and more likely to be remembered. As a by-product of organizing the communication, you also create more appealing (more organized) *white space* (designers' favorite term).

How to get it

Squint your eyes slightly and count the number of visual elements on the page by counting the number of times your eye stops. If there are more than three to five items on the page (of course it depends on the piece), see which of the separate elements can be grouped together into closer proximity to become one visual unit.

What to avoid

Avoid too many separate elements on a page.

Don't stick things in the corners and in the middle.

Avoid leaving equal amounts of white space between elements unless each group is part of a subset (see the example on page 21).

Avoid even a split second of confusion over whether a headline, a subhead, a caption, a graphic, etc., belongs with its related material. Create a relationship among elements with close proximity.

Don't create relationships with elements that don't belong together! If they are not *related*, move them apart from each other.

Alignment

Design beginners tend to put text and graphics on the page wherever there happens to be space, often without regard to any other items on the page. What this creates is the slightly-messy-kitchen effect—you know, with a cup here, a plate there, a napkin on the floor, a pot in the sink, a spill on the floor. It doesn't take much to clean up the slightly messy kitchen, just as it doesn't take much to clean up a slighty messy design that has weak alignments.

The principle of alignment states that **nothing should be placed on the page arbitrarily. Every item should have a visual connection with something else on the page.** The principle of alignment forces you to be more conscious—no longer can you just throw things on the page wherever there happens to be room.

When items are aligned on the page, it creates a stronger cohesive unit. Even when elements are physically separated from each other, if they are aligned there is an invisible line that connects them, both in your eye and in your mind. Although you might have separated certain elements to indicate their relationships (following the principle of proximity), the principle of alignment is what tells the reader that even though these items are not close, they belong to the same piece. The following pages illustrate this idea.

Take a look at this business card, the same one you saw in the last chapter. Part of its problem is that nothing is aligned with anything else. In this little space, there are elements aligned to the left edge, the right edge, and the center. Neither the text in the upper two corners or the bottom two corners are aligned across on the same baseline, nor are they aligned on the left or right edges.

◀ The elements on this card look like they were just thrown on and stuck. Not one of the elements has any connection with any other element on the card.

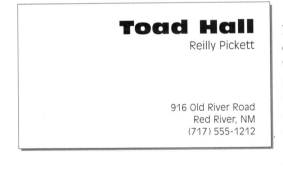

◀ By moving all the elements over to the right and giving them one alignment, the information is instantly more organized. (Of course, you realize I also grouped related elements into closer proximity.)

The text items now have a common boundary, connecting them together.

In the example (repeated below) that you saw in the proximity section, the text is also aligned—it's aligned down the center. But if text is aligned, instead, on the left or the right, the invisible line that connects the text is much stronger because it has a hard vertical edge to follow. This gives left- and right-aligned text a cleaner and more dramatic look. Compare the two examples below, then we'll talk about it on the following pages.

This example has a nice arrangement with the text items grouped into logical proximity. The text is center-aligned over itself, and centered on the page.

▶

Toad Hall

Reilly Pickett

916 Old River Road
Red River, NM
(717) 555-1212

This has the same logical arrangement, but it is now right-aligned. Can you see the hard edge on the right? There is a stronger invisible line connecting the edges of these two groups of text than there is in the centered alignment, above.

▶

Toad Hall

Reilly Pickett

916 Old River Road
Red River, NM
(717) 555-1212

▲

The invisible line runs right down here, connecting the text.

Do you tend to automatically center everything? A centered alignment is the most common alignment that beginners use—it's very safe, it feels comfortable. A centered alignment creates a more formal look, a more sedate look, a more ordinary and oftentimes downright dull look. Take notice of the designs you like. I guarantee that most designs that have a sophisticated look are not centered. I know it's difficult, as a beginner, to break away from a centered alignment; you'll have to force yourself to do it at first. But combine a strong flush right or left alignment with good use of proximity and you will be amazed at the change in your work.

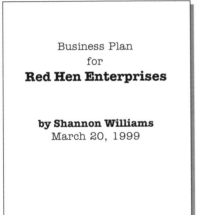

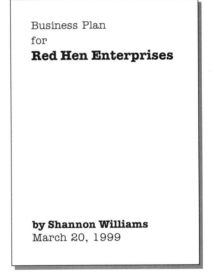

▲ This is a typical report cover, yes? This standard format presents a dull, almost amateurish look, which may influence someone's initial reaction to the report.

▲ The strong flush-left alignment gives the report cover a more sophisticated impression. Even though the author's name is far from the title, that invisible line of the strong alignment connects the two text blocks.

I'm not suggesting that you *never* center anything! Just be conscious of the effect a centered alignment has—is that really the look you want to portray? Sometimes it is; for instance, most weddings are rather sedate, formal affairs, so if you want to center your wedding announcement, do so consciously and joyfully.

Sometimes you can add a bit of a twist on the centered arrangement, such as centering the type, but setting the block of type itself off center. Or set the type high on the page to create more tension. Or set a very casual, fun typeface in a very formal, centered arrangement.

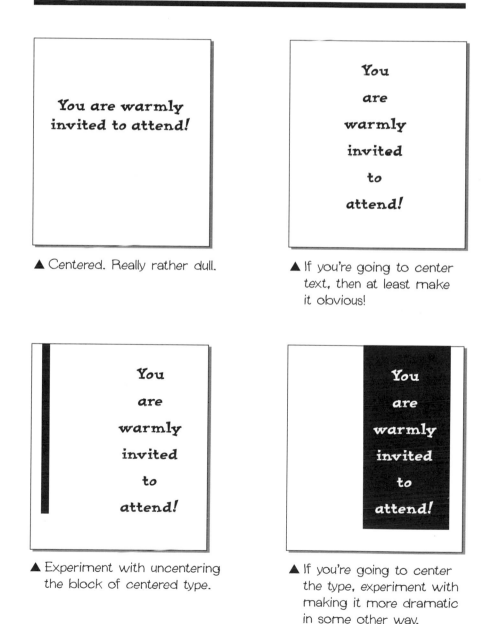

▲ Centered. Really rather dull.

▲ If you're going to center text, then at least make it obvious!

▲ Experiment with uncentering the block of centered type.

▲ If you're going to center the type, experiment with making it more dramatic in some other way.

You're accustomed to working with text alignments. Until you have more training, stick to the guideline of using one text alignment on the page: either all text is flush left, flush right, or centered.

This text is **flush left.** Some people call it quad left, or you can say it is left aligned.

This text is **flush right.** Some people call it quad right, or you can say it is right aligned.

This text is **centered.**
If you are going to
center text,
make it obvious.

See, in this paragraph it is
difficult to tell if this text
was centered purposely
or perhaps accidentally.
The line lengths are not
the same, but they are not
really different. If you can't
instantly tell that the type
is centered, why bother?

This text is **justified.** Some people call it quad left and right, and some call it blocked—the text lines up on both sides. Whatever you call it, don't do it unless your line length is long enough to avoid awkward gaps   between   the   words.

Occasionally you can get away with using both flush right and flush left text on the same page, but make sure you align them in some way!

▶

In this example, the title and the subtitle are flush left, but the description is centered— there is no common alignment between the two elements of text. They don't have any connection to each other.

> # **Robert Burns**
> *Poems in Scots*
> *and English*
>
>
>
>
> The most
> complete edition
> available of
> Scotland's greatest
> lyric poet.

▶

Although these two elements still have two different alignments (the top is flush left and the bottom is flush right), the edge of the descriptive text below aligns with the right edge of the title above, connecting the elements with an invisible line. This was not an accident!

> # **Robert Burns**
> *Poems in Scots*
> *and English*
>
>
>
>
> The most
> complete edition
> available of
> Scotland's greatest
> lyric poet.

When you place other items on the page, make sure each one has some visual alignment with another item on the page. If lines of text are across from each other horizontally, align their baselines. If there are several separate blocks of text, align their left or right edges. If there are graphic elements, align their edges with other edges on the page. Nothing should be placed on the page arbitrarily!

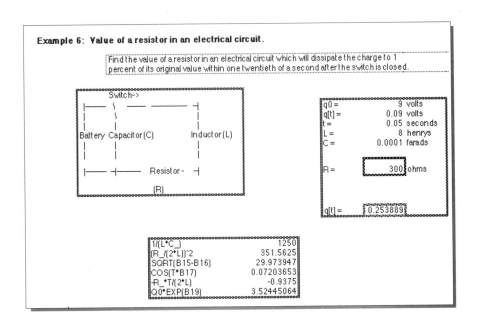

Example 6: Value of a resistor in an electrical circuit.

▲ Even though it may be a boring ol' spreadsheet, there is no reason not to make the page look as nice as possible, and to present the information as clearly as possible. There are two problems here, right? A lack of proximity and a lack of alignment.

Lack of alignment is probably the biggest cause of unpleasant-looking documents. Our eyes *like* to see order; it creates a calm, secure feeling.

In any well-designed piece, you will be able to draw lines to the aligned objects, even if the overall presentation of material is a wild collection of odd things and has lots of energy.

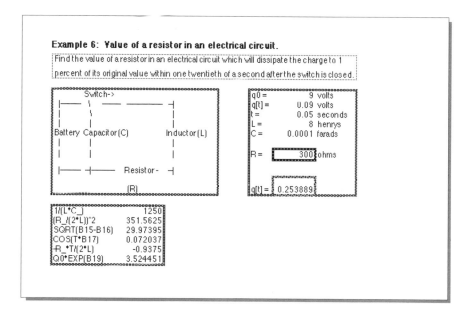

Example 6: Value of a resistor in an electrical circuit.

Find the value of a resistor in an electrical circuit which will dissipate the charge to 1 percent of its original value within one twentieth of a second after the switch is closed.

▲ Simply lining things up makes all the difference here. Notice not one item is on the page arbitrarily—every item has some visual connection with another item on the page.

If I knew what this spreadsheet was talking about, I might choose to move the square chart on the right over to the left, closer to the big chart, keeping their tops aligned, and not worry about aligning the square chart with the right edge. If I did move it over, I would adjust the spacing between the three charts acccording to their intellectual relationships to each other.

A problem with many non–designers' publications is a *subtle* lack of alignment, such as centered headlines and subheads over indented paragraphs. At first glance, which of the examples on these two pages presents a cleaner and sharper image?

Honor Form

Heresy rheumatic starry offer former's dodder, Violate Huskings, an wart hoppings darn honor form.

Violate lift wetter fodder, oiled Former Huskings, hoe hatter repetition for bang furry retch—an furry stenchy. Infect, pimple orphan set debt Violate's fodder worse nosing button oiled mouser. Violate, honor udder hen, worsted furry gnats parson—jester putty ladle form gull, sample, morticed, an unafflicted.

Tarred gull

Wan moaning Former Huskings nudist haze dodder setting honor cheer, during nosing.

"Violate!" sorted dole former, "Watcher setting darn fur? Denture nor yore canned gat retch setting darn during nosing? Germ pup otter debt cheer!"

"Arm tarred, Fodder," resplendent Violate warily.

"Watcher tarred fur?" aster stenchy former, hoe dint half mush symphony further gull.

Feeder pegs

"Are badger dint doe mush woke disk moaning! Ditcher curry doze buckles fuller slob darn tutor peg-pan an feeder pegs?"

"Yap, Fodder. Are fetter pegs."

"Ditcher mail-car caws an swoop otter caw staple?" "Off curse, Fodder. Are mulct oiler caws an swapped otter staple, fetter checkings, an clammed upper larder inner checking-horse toe gadder

▲ This is a very common sight: headlines are centered, text is flush left, paragraph indents are "typewriter" wide (that is, five spaces or half-an-inch, as you learned in high school), the "photo-graph" is centered in a column.

▶ Never center headlines over flush left body copy or text that has an indent. If the text does not have a clear left and right edge, you can't tell the headline is actually centered. It looks like it's just hanging around.

All these unaligned spots create a messy page: wide indents, ragged right edge of text, centered heads with open space on both sides, centered photo.

All those minor misalignments add up to create a visually messy page. Find a strong line and stick to it. Even though it may be subtle and your boss couldn't say what made the difference between this example and the one before it, the more sophisticated look comes through clearly.

Honor Form

Heresy rheumatic starry offer former's dodder, Violate Huskings, an wart hoppings darn honor form.

Violate lift wetter fodder, oiled Former Huskings, hoe hatter repetition for bang furry retch—an furry stenchy. Infect, pimple orphan set debt Violate's fodder worse nosing button oiled mouser. Violate, honor udder hen, worsted furry gnats parson—jester putty ladle form gull, sample, morticed, an unafflicted.

Tarred gull

Wan moaning Former Huskings nudist haze dodder setting honor cheer, during nosing.

"Violate!" sorted dole former, "Watcher setting darn fur? Denture nor yore canned gat retch setting darn during nosing? Germ pup otter debt cheer!"

"Arm tarred, Fodder," resplendent Violate warily.

"Watcher tarred fur?" aster stenchy former, hoe dint half mush symphony further gull.

Feeder pegs

"Are badger dint doe mush woke disk moaning! Ditcher curry doze buckles fuller slob darn tutor peg-pan an feeder pegs?"

"Yap, Fodder. Are fetter pegs."

"Ditcher mail-car caws an swoop otter caw staple?" "Off curse, Fodder. Are mulct oiler caws an swapped otter staple, fetter checkings, an clammed upper larder inner checking-horse toe gadder oiler aches, an wen darn tutor vestibule guarding two peck oiler bogs

▲ Find a strong alignment and stick to it. If the text is flush left, set the heads and subheads flush left.

First paragraphs are traditionally not indented. The purpose of indenting a paragraph is to tell you there is a new paragraph, but you always know the first one is a paragraph.

On a typewriter, you indented five spaces. With proportional type such as you are using on your computer, the standard typographic indent is one em (an em is as wide as the point size of your type), which is more like two spaces.

Be conscious of the ragged edge of your type. Adjust the lines so your right edge is as smooth as possible.

If there are photographs or illustrations, align them with an edge and/or a baseline.

Even in a piece that has a good start on a nice design, the subtle lack of alignment is often the missing key to a more professional look.

Ladle Rat Rotten Hut

The story of a wicket woof and a ladle gull.

by H. Chace

Wants pawn term, dare worsted ladle gull hoe lift wetter murder inner ladle cordage, honor itch offer lodge, dock, florist. Disk ladle gull orphan worry putty ladle rat cluck wetter ladle rat hut, an fur disk raisin pimple colder Ladle Rat Rotten Hut.

Wan moaning, Ladle Rat Rotten Hut's murder colder inset. "Ladle Rat Rotten Hut, heresy ladle basking winsome burden barter an shirker cockles. Tick disk ladle basking tutor cordage offer groin-murder hoe lifts honor udder site offer florist. Shaker lake! Dun stopper laundry wrote! Dun stopper peck floors! Dun daily-doily inner florist, an yonder nor sorghum-stenches, dun stopper torque wet strainers!"

"Hoe-cake, murder," resplendent Ladle Rotten Hut, an tickle ladle basking an stuttered oft. Honor wrote tutor cordage offer groin-murder, Ladle Rat Rotten Hut mitten anomalous woof.

"Wail, wail, wail!" set disk wicket woof, "Evanescent Ladle Rat Rotten Hut! Wares are putty ladle gull goring wizard ladle basking?"

"Armor goring tumor groin-murder's," reprisal ladle gull. "Grammar's seeking bet. Armor ticking arson burden barter an shirker cockles."

"O hoe! Heifer gnats woke," setter wicket woof, butter taught tomb shelf, "Oil tickle shirt court tutor cordage offer groin-murder. Oil ketchup wetter letter, an den—O bore!"

Soda wicket woof tucker shirt court, an whinney retched a cordage offer groin-murder, picked inner windrow, an sore debtor pore oil worming worse lion inner bet. En inner flesh, disk abdominal woof lipped honor bet, paunched honor pore oil worming, an garbled erupt. Den disk ratchet ammonol pot honor groin-murder's nut cup and gnat-gun, any curdled ope inner bet.

Inner ladle wile, Ladle Rat Rotten Hut a raft attar cordage, an ranker dough ball. "Comb ink, sweat hard," setter wicket woof, disgracing is verse. Ladle Rat Rotten Hut entity bet-rum an stud buyer groin-murder's bet.

"O Grammar!" crater ladle gull historically, "Water bag icer gut! A nervous sausage bag ice!"

"Battered lucky chew whiff, sweat hard," setter bloat-Thursday woof, wetter wicket small honors phase.

"O Grammar, water bag noise! A nervous sore suture anomolous prognosis!"

"Battered small your whiff, doling," whiskered dole woof, ants mouse worse waddling.

"O Grammar, water bag mouser gut! A nervous sore suture bag mouse!"

Daze worry on-forger-nut ladle gull's lest warts. Oil offer sodden, caking offer carvers an sprinkling otter bet, disk hoard-hoarded woof lipped own pore Ladle Rat Rotten Hut an garbled erupt.

—H. Chace
Anguish Languish

Mural: Yonder nor sorghum-stenches shut ladle gulls stopper torque wet strainers.

▲ Can you see all the places where items could be aligned, but aren't? If this is your book, go ahead and circle all the misalignments on this page. There are at least nine!

Check for illustrations that hang out over the edge just a bit, or captions that are centered under photos, or headlines that are not aligned with the text, or a combination of centered text and flush left text.

Ladle Rat Rotten Hut

The story of a wicket woof and a ladle gull.   by H. Chace

Wants pawn term, dare worsted ladle gull hoe lift wetter murder inner ladle cordage, honor itch offer lodge, dock, florist. Disk ladle gull orphan worry putty ladle rat cluck wetter ladle rat hut, an fur disk raisin pimplo oolder Ladle Rat Rotten Hut.

Wan moaning, Ladle Rat Rotten Hut's murder colder inset. "Ladle Rat Rotten Hut, heresy ladle basking winsome burden barter an shirker cockles. Tick disk ladle basking tutor cordage offer groinmurder hoe lifts honor udder site offer florist. Shaker lake! Dun stopper laundry wrote! Dun stopper peck floors! Dun daily-doily inner florist, an yonder nor sorghum-stenches, dun stopper torque wet strainers!"

"Hoe-cake, murder," resplendent Ladle Rat Rotten Hut, an tickle ladle basking an stuttered oft. Honor wrote tutor cordage offer groin-murder, Ladle Rat Rotten Hut mitten anomalous woof.

"Wail, wail, wail!" set disk wicket woof, "Evanescent Ladle Rat Rotten Hut! Wares are putty ladle gull goring wizard ladle basking?"

"Armor goring tumor groin-murder's," reprisal ladle gull. "Grammar's seeking bet. Armor ticking arson burden barter an shirker cockles."

"O hoe! Heifer gnats woke," setter wicket woof, butter taught tomb shelf, "Oil tickle shirt court tutor cordage offer groin-murder. Oil ketchup wetter letter, an den—O bore!"

Soda wicket woof tucker shirt court, an whinney retched a cordage offer groin-murder, picked inner windrow, an sore debtor pore oil worming worse lion inner bet. En inner flesh, disk abdominal woof lipped honor bet, paunched honor pore oil worming, an garbled erupt. Den disk ratchet ammonol pot honor groin-murder's nut cup and gnat-gun, any curdled ope inner bet.

Inner ladle wile, Ladle Rat Rotten Hut, a raft attar cordage, an ranker dough ball. "Comb ink, sweat hard," setter wicket woof, disgracing is verse. Ladle Rat Rotten Hut entity bet-rum an stud buyer groin-murder's bet.

"O Grammar!" crater ladle gull historically, "Water bag icer gut! A nervous sausage bag ice!"

"Battered lucky chew whiff, sweat hard," setter bloat-Thursday woof, wetter wicket small honors phase.

"O Grammar, water bag noise! A nervous sore suture anomolous prognosis!"

"Battered small your whiff, doling," whiskered dole woof, ants mouse worse waddling.

"O Grammar, water bag mouser gut! A nervous sore suture bag mouse!"

Daze worry on-forger-nut ladle gull's lest warts. Oil offer sodden, caking offer carvers an sprinkling otter bet, disk hoard-hoarded woof lipped own pore Ladle Rat Rotten Hut an garbled erupt.

—H. Chace
Anguish Languish

Mural: Yonder nor sorghum-stenches shut ladle gulls stopper torque wet strainers.

▲ Can you see now what has made the difference between this example and the one on the previous page? If this is your book, go ahead and draw lines along the strong alignments.

I want to repeat: find a strong line and use it. If you have a photo or a graphic with a strong flush side, align the flush side of the text along the straight edge of the photo, as shown below.

Center Alley

Center Alley worse jester pore ladle gull hoe lift wetter stop-murder an toe heft-cisterns. Daze worming war furry wicket an shellfish parsons, spatially dole stop-murder, hoe dint lack Center Alley an, infect, word orphan traitor pore gull mar lichen ammonol dinner hormone bang.

Center Alley's furry gourd-murder whiskered, "Watcher crane aboard?"

▲ There is a nice strong line here along the edge of the type. There is a nice strong line along the edge of the "photograph." Between the text and the photo, though, there is "trapped" white space, and the white space is an awkward shape. When white space is trapped, it pushes the two elements apart.

Center Alley

Center Alley worse jester pore ladle gull hoe lift wetter stop-murder an toe heft-cisterns. Daze worming war furry wicket an shellfish parsons, spatially dole stop-murder, hoe dint lack Center Alley an, infect, word orphan traitor pore gull mar lichen ammonol dinner hormone bang.

Center Alley's furry gourd-murder whiskered, "Watcher crane aboard?"

▲ "Find a strong line and use it." Now the strong line of the text and the strong line of the photograph are next to each other, making each other stronger. The white space now is floating free off the left edge. The caption has also been set against the same strong line of the edge of the photo.

If your alignments are strong, then you can break through the alignments *consciously* and it will look intentional. What a concept.

Guilty Looks Enter Tree Beers

Wants pawn term dare worsted ladle gull hoe hat search putty yowler coils debt pimple colder Guilty Looks. Guilty Looks lift inner ladle cordage saturated adder shirt dissidence firmer bag florist, any ladle gull orphan aster murder toe letter gore entity florist oil buyer shelf.

Debt florist's mush toe dentures furry ladle gull.

"Guilty Looks!" crater murder angularly. "Hominy terms area garner asthma suture stooped quizchin? Goiter door florist? Sordidly NUT!"

"Wire nut, murder?" wined Guilty Looks, hoe dint peony tension tore murder's scaldings. "Cause dorsal lodge an wicket beer inner florist live orphan molasses pimple. Ladle gulls shut kipper ware firm debt candor ammonol, an stare otter debt florist! Debt florist's mush toe dentures furry ladle gull!"

Hormone nurture

Wail, pimple oil-wares wander doe wart udder pimple dun wampum toe doe. Debt's jest hormone nurture. Wan moaning, Guilty Looks dissipater murder, an win entity florist. Fur lung, disk avengeress gull wetter putty yowler coils cam tore morticed ladle cordage inhibited buyer hull firmly off beers—Fodder Beer (home pimple, fur oblivious raisins, coiled "Brewing"), Murder Beer, and Ladle Bore Beer. Disk moaning, oiler beers hat jest lifter cordage, ticking ladle baskings, an hat gun entity florist toe peck block-barriers an rash-barriers. Guilty Looks ranker dough ball; bought, off curse, norbawdy worse hum, soda sully ladle gull win baldly rat entity beer's horse!

Sop's toe hart

Honor tipple inner darning rum, stud tree boils fuller sop—wan grade bag boiler sop, wan muddle-sash boil, an wan tawny ladle boil. Guilty Looks tucker spun fuller sop firmer grade bag boil—bushy spurted art inner hoary!

▲ Well, I *tried* not to align it (but I'm too programmed). Even though that inset piece is breaking into the text block, can you see where it is aligned on the left? It is possible to sometimes break completely free of any alignment, *if you do it consciously.*

▶ I am giving you a number of rules here, but it is true that rules are made to be broken. There is a rule, though, about breaking rules: you must know what the rule *is* before you can break it.

Summary of Alignment

Nothing should be placed on the page arbitrarily. Every element should have some visual connection with another element on the page.

Unity is an important concept in design. To make all the elements on the page appear to be unified, connected, and interrelated, there needs to be some visual tie between the separate elements. Even if the separate elements are not physically close on the page, they can *appear* connected, related, unified with the other information simply by their placement. Take a look at designs you like. No matter how wild and chaotic a well-designed piece may initially appear, you can always find the alignments within.

The basic purpose

The basic purpose of alignment is to unify and organize the page. The result is kind of like what happens when you pick up all the baby toys that were strewn around the living room floor and put them all into one toy box.

It is often a strong alignment (combined, of course, with the appropriate typeface) that creates a sophisticated look, or a formal look, a fun look, or a serious look.

How to get it

Be conscious of where you place elements. Always find something else on the page to align with, even if the two objects are physically far away from each other.

What to avoid

Avoid using more than one text alignment on the page (that is, don't center some text and right-align other text).

And please try very hard to break away from a centered alignment unless you are consciously trying to create a more formal, sedate (often dull?) presentation. Choose a centered alignment consciously, not by default.

Repetition

The principle of repetition states that you **repeat some aspect of the design throughout the entire piece.** The repetitive element may be a bold font, a thick rule (line), a certain bullet, color, design element, particular format, spatial relationships, etc. It can be anything that a reader will visually recognize.

You already use repetition in your work. When you make headlines all the same size and weight, when you add a rule a half-inch from the bottom of each page, when you use the same bullet in each list throughout the project—these are all examples of repetition. What beginners often need to do is push this idea further—turn that inconspicuous repetition into a visual key that ties the publication together.

Repetition can be thought of as "consistency." As you look through an eight-page newsletter, it is the repetition of certain elements, their consistency, that makes each of those eight pages appear to belong to the same newsletter. If page 7 has no repetitive elements carried over from page 6, then the entire newsletter loses its cohesive look and feel.

But repetition goes beyond just being naturally consistent—it is a conscious effort to unify all parts of a design.

Here is the same business card we worked with earlier. In the second example, I have added a repetitive element, the strong, bold typeface. Take a look at it, and notice where your eye moves. When you get to the phone number, where do you look next? Do you go back to the beginning, the other bold type? This is a visual trick designers have always used to control a reader's eye, to keep your attention on the page as long as possible.

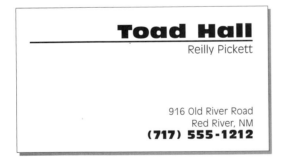

Toad Hall
Reilly Pickett

916 Old River Road
Red River, NM
(717) 555-1212

◄ When you get to the end of the information, does your eye just wander off the card?

Toad Hall
Reilly Pickett

916 Old River Road
Red River, NM
(717) 555-1212

◄ Now when you get to the end of the information, where does your eye go? Do you find that it bounces back and forth between the bold type elements?

Take advantage of those elements you're already using to make a project consistent and turn those elements into repetitive graphic symbols. Are all the headlines in your newsletter 14-point Times Bold? How about investing in a very bold sans serif face and making all your heads something like 16-point Antique Olive Black? Not only is your page more visually interesting, but you also increase the visual organization and the consistency by making it more obvious. You're taking the repetition you have already built into the project and pushing it so it is stronger and more dynamic.

Guilty Looks

Wants pawn term dare worsted ladle gull hoe hat search putty yowler coils debt pimple colder Guilty Looks. Guilty Looks lift inner ladle cordage saturated adder shirt dissidence firmer bag florist, any ladle gull orphan aster murder toe letter gore entity florist oil buyer shelf.

"Guilty Looks!" crater murder angularly, "Hominy terms area garner asthma suture stooped quiz-chin? Goiter door florist? Sordidly NUT!"

Wire nut?

"Wire nut, murder?" wined Guilty Looks, hoe dint peony tension tore murder's scaldings.

"Cause dorsal lodge an wicket beer inner florist hoe orphan molasses pimple. Ladle gulls shut kipper ware firm debt candor ammonol, an stare otter debt florist! Debt florist's mush toe dentures furry ladle gull!"

Hormone nurture

Wail, pimple oil-wares wander doe wart udder pimple dun wampum toe doe. Debt's jest hormone nurture. Wan moaning, Guilty Looks dissipater murder, an win entity florist.

Tree Beers

Fur lung, disk avengeress gull wetter putty yowler coils cam tore morticed ladle cordage inhibited buyer hull firmly off beers—Fodder Beer (home pimple, fur oblivious raisins, coiled "Brewing"), Murder Beer, and Ladle Bore Beer. Disk moaning, oiler beers hat jest lifter cordage, ticking ladle

▲ Headlines and subheads are a good place to start for creating repetitive elements, since you are probably consistent with them anyway.

Guilty Looks

Wants pawn term dare worsted ladle gull hoe hat search putty yowler coils debt pimple colder Guilty Looks. Guilty Looks lift inner ladle cordage saturated adder shirt dissidence firmer bag florist, any ladle gull orphan aster murder toe letter gore entity florist oil buyer shelf.

"Guilty Looks!" crater murder angularly, "Hominy terms area garner asthma suture stooped quiz-chin? Goiter door florist? Sordidly NUT!"

Wire nut?

"Wire nut, murder?" wined Guilty Looks, hoe dint peony tension tore murder's scaldings.

"Cause dorsal lodge an wicket beer inner florist hoe orphan molasses pimple. Ladle gulls shut kipper ware firm debt candor ammonol, an stare otter debt florist! Debt florist's mush toe dentures furry ladle gull!"

Hormone nurture

Wail, pimple oil-wares wander doe wart udder pimple dun wampum toe doe. Debt's jest hormone nurture. Wan moaning, Guilty Looks dissipater murder, an win entity florist.

Tree Beers

Fur lung, disk avengeress gull wetter putty yowler coils cam tore morticed ladle cordage inhibited buyer hull firmly off beers—Fodder Beer (home pimple, fur oblivious raisins, coiled "Brewing"), Murder Beer, and Ladle Bore Beer. Disk moaning, oiler beers hat jest lifter cordage, ticking ladle

▲ So take that consistent element and make it stronger.

Do you create multiple-page publications? Repetition is a major factor in the unity of those pages. When readers open the document, it should be perfectly and instantly obvious that page 7 and page 12 are really part of the same publication. The two pages shown below and to the right are part of one publication. Can you point out all the elements of repetition?

▶ Consistent double rule on all pages.

▶ Consistent typeface in headlines and subheads, and consistent space above each.

Single rule repeats across bottom of each page.

▶ Page numbers are in the same place, same typeface, on each page.

Darn Honor Form

Heresy rheumatic starry offer former's dodder, Violate Huskings, an wart hoppings darn honor form.

Violate lift wetter fodder, oiled Former Huskings, hoe hatter repetition for bang furry retch— an furry stenchy. Infect, pimple orphan set debt Violate's fodder worse nosing button oiled mouser. Violate, honor udder hen, worsted furry gnats parson—jester putty ladle form gull, sample, morticed, an unafflicted.

Wan moaning Former Huskings nudist haze dodder setting honor cheer, during nosing.

Nor symphony

"Violate!" sorted dole former, "Watcher setting darn fur? Yore canned gat retch setting darn during nosing? Germ pup otter debt cheer!"

"Arm tarred, Fodder," resplendent Violate warily.

"Watcher tarred fur?" aster stenchy former, hoe dint half mush symphony further gull. "Are badger dint doe mush woke disk moaning! Ditcher curry doze buckles fuller slob darn tutor peg-pan an feeder pegs?"

▶ *A caption for this photo.*

Vestibule guardings

"Yap, Fodder. Are fetter pegs."

"Ditcher mail-car caws an swoop otter caw staple?" "Off curse, Fodder. Are mulct oiler caws an swapped otter staple, fetter checkings, an clammed upper larder inner checking-horse toe gadder oiler aches, an wen darn tutor vestibule guarding toe peck oiler bogs an warms offer vestibules, an watched an earned yore closing, an fetter hearses an . . ."

"Ditcher *warder* oiler hearses, toe?" enter-ruptured oiled Huskings.

"Nor, Fodder, are dint."

"Dint warder mar hearses? Wire nut?"

4

▲ The text has a "bottoming out" point, but not all text must align here *if there is a consistent, repetitive starting point at the top of the page.*

Some publications might choose to repetitively bottom out rather than "hang from a clothesline" (align across the top). One or the other technique should be consistent, though.

If you have a strongly consistent publication, you can get away with some surprise elements. I'd suggest you save those surprises for items you want to call special attention to.

Can you point out the consistent, repetitive elements of this book?

◀ All stories and photos or illustrations start at the same guideline across the top of each page (also see note below, left).

◀ The single, wide column takes up the same space as two columns, maintaining the consistency of the outer borders.

▲ Note the repetitive use of the triangular shape in the list and in the caption, opposite page. That shape is probably used elsewhere in the publication as well.

To create a consistent business package with a business card, letterhead, and envelope, use a strong display of repetition, not only within each piece, but between all the pieces. You want the person who receives the letter to know you are the same person who gave them a business card last week. And create a layout that allows you to align the printed letter with some element in the stationery design!

RED HEN

Shannon
Williams

◄You can see that a letter typed with a solid left alignment would create a strong impression on this page.

Route 9

Box 16

San Gelato

Arizona

87776

123.456.7890

RED HEN

Shannon
Williams

Route 9

Box 16

San Gelato

Arizona

87776

123.456.7890

RED HEN

Route 9

Box 16

San Gelato

Arizona

87776

Repetition helps organize the information; it helps guide the reader through the pages; it helps unify disparate parts of the design. Even on a one-page document, repetitive elements establish a sophisticated continuity. If you are creating several one-page documents that are part of a comprehensive package, it is critical that you employ repetition.

▶

Repetitions:
Bold typeface
Light typeface
Square bullets
Indents
Spacing
Alignments

Mickey Mouse
- Walt Disney Studios
  Anaheim, California
  58 years old, no children

Employment
- Walt Disney Studios
- Various television studios

Education
- Walt Disney Studios

Favorite Activities
- Driving steamboats
- Roping cattle

Favorite Quote
- Everybody can't be a duck.

▲ Besides having strong repetitive elements that make it very clear exactly what is going on here, Mickey might also want to incorporate one or more of these elements into the design of his cover letter.

If there is an element that strikes a fancy with you, go with it! Perhaps it is a piece of clip art or a picture font. Feel free to add something completely new simply for the purpose of repetition. Or take a simple element and use it in various ways—different sizes, colors, angles.

Sometimes the repeated items are not *exactly* the same objects, but objects so closely related that their connection is very clear.

It's
a
wild
tea
party!

please join us
may 1
3 o'clock
in the
afternoon
wear
your
hat

▲ It's fun and *effective* to pull an element out of a graphic and repeat it. This little triangular motif could be applied to other related material, such as envelopes, response cards, balloons, *etc.*, and everything would be a cohesive unit, *even* without repeating the whole teapot.

Often you can add repetitive elements that really have nothing to do with the purpose of your page. For instance, throw in a few petroglyph characters on a survey form. Add some strange-looking birds to a report. Set several particularly beautiful characters in your font in various large sizes, in gray or a light second color, and at various angles throughout the publication. It's okay to have fun!

Grand Opening
Sale
at
PickWick Papers!

paper
envelopes
rubber stamps
glitter
fancy stickers

Fort Marcy Center • Friday • May 7

▲ Pulling a design element outside of the borders serves to unify two or more pieces, or to unify a foreground and a background, or to unify separate publications that have a common theme. Notice how the "poster" and this page seem to be connected because of the repetition of primitive characters.

Summary of Repetition

A repetition of visual elements throughout the design unifies and strengthens a piece by tying together otherwise separate parts. Repetition is very useful on one-page pieces, and is critical in multi-page documents (where we often just call it *being consistent*).

The basic purpose

The purpose of repetition is to unify and to add visual interest. Don't underestimate the visual interest of a page—if a piece looks interesting, it is more likely to be read.

How to get it

Think of repetition as being consistent, which I'm sure you are already. Then push the existing consistencies a little further—can you turn some of those consistent elements into part of the conscious graphic design, as with the headline? Do you use a 1-point rule at the bottom of each page or under each heading? How about using a 4-point rule instead to make the repetitive element stronger and more dramatic?

Then take a look at the possibility of adding elements just to create a repetition. Do you have a numbered list of items? How about using a distinctive font or a reversed number, and then repeating that treatment throughout every numbered list in the publication? At first, simply find *existing* repetitions and then strengthen them. As you get used to the idea and the look, start to *create* repetitions to enhance the design and the clarity of the information.

Repetition is like accenting your clothes. If a woman is wearing a lovely black evening dress with a chic black hat, she might accent her dress with red heels, red lipstick, and a tiny red rose corsage.

What to avoid

Avoid repeating the element so much that it becomes annoying or over-whelming. Be concious of the value of contrast (read the next chapter and the section on contrasting type).

For instance, if she were to wear the black evening dress with a red hat, red earrings, red lipstick, a red handbag, red shoes and a red coat, the repetition would not be a stunning and unifying contrast—it would be garish and the focus would be confused.

Contrast

Contrast is one of the most effective ways to add visual interest to your page—a striking interest that makes you want to look at the page—and to create an organizational hierarchy among different elements. The important "rule" to remember is that for contrast to be effective, it must be strong. Don't be a wimp.

Contrast is created when two elements are different. If the two elements are sort of different, but not really, then you don't have contrast, you have conflict. That's the key—the principle of contrast states that **if two items are not exactly the same, then make them different. Really different.**

Contrast can be created in many ways. You can contrast large type with small type; a graceful oldstyle font with a bold sans serif font; a thin line with a thick line; a cool color with a warm color; a smooth texture with a rough texture; a horizontal element (such as a long line of text) with a vertical element (such as a tall, narrow column of text); widely spaced lines with closely packed lines; a small graphic with a large graphic.

Just don't be a wimp. You cannot contrast 12-point type with 14-point type. You cannot contrast a half-point rule with a one-point rule. You cannot contrast dark brown with black. Get serious.

If the two "newsletters" below came across your desk, which one would you read first? They both have the same basic layout. They are both nice and neat. They both have the same information on the page. There is really only one difference: the newsletter on the right has more contrast.

ANOTHER NEWSLETTER!

January   First   1994

Exciting Headline

Wants pawn term dare worsted ladle gull hoe hat search putty yowler coils debt pimple colder Guilty Looks. Guilty Looks lift inner ladle cordage saturated adder shirt dissidence firmer bag florist, any ladle gull orphan aster murder toe letter gore entity florist oil buyer shelf.

Thrilling Subhead

"Guilty Looks!" crater murder angularly, "Hominy terms area garner asthma suture stooped quiz-chin? Goiter door florist? Sordidly NUT!"

"Wire nut, murder?" wined Guilty Looks, hoe dint peony tension tore murder's scaldings.

"Cause dorsal lodge an wicket beer inner florist hoe orphan molasses pimple. Ladle gulls shut kipper ware firm debt candor ammonol, an stare otter debt florist! Debt florist's mush toe dentures furry ladle gull!"

Another Exciting Headline

Wail, pimple oil-wares wander doe wart udder pimple dun wampum toe doe. Debt's jest hormone nurture. Wan moaning, Guilty Looks dissipater murder, an win entity florist.

Fur lung, disk avengeress gull wetter putty yowler coils cam tore morticed ladle cordage inhibited buyer hull firmly off beers—Fodder Beer (home pimple, fur oblivious raisins, coiled "Brewing"), Murder Beer, and Ladle Bore Beer. Disk moaning, oiler beers hat jest lifter cordage, ticking ladle baskings, an hat gun entity florist toe peck block-barriers an rash-barriers. Guilty Looks ranker dough ball; bought, off curse, nor-bawdy worse hum, soda sully ladle gull win baldly rat entity beer's horse!

Boring Subhead

Honor tipple inner darning rum, stud tree boils fuller sop—wan grade bag boiler sop, wan muddle-sash boil, an wan tawny ladle boil. Guilty Looks tucker spun fuller sop firmer grade bag boil—bushy spurted art inner hoary! "Arch," crater gull, "Deb sop's tpe hart—barns mar mouse!"

Dingy traitor sop inner muddle-sash boil, witch worse to coiled. Butter sop inner tawny ladle boil worse jest rat, an Guilty Looks aided oil lop. Dingy nudist tree cheers—wan anomalous cheer, wan muddle-sash

▲ This is nice and neat, but there is nothing that attracts your eyes to it.

The cause of the contrast is obvious. I used a stronger, bolder typeface in the headlines and subheads. I repeated that typeface (principle of repetition, remember?) in the newsletter title. Because I changed the title from all caps to caps/lowercase, I was able to use a larger and bolder type size, which also helps reinforce the contrast. And because the headlines are so strong now, I could add a dark band across the top behind the title, again repeating the dark color and reinforcing the contrast.

Another Newsletter!

January First 1998

Exciting Headline

Wants pawn term dare worsted ladle gull hoe hat search putty yowler coils debt pimple colder Guilty Looks. Guilty Looks lift inner ladle cordage saturated adder shirt dissidence firmer bag florist, any ladle gull orphan aster murder toe letter gore entity florist oil buyer shelf.

Thrilling Subhead

"Guilty Looks!" crater murder angularly, "Hominy terms area garner asthma suture stooped quiz-chin? Goiter door florist? Sordidly NUT!"

"Wire nut, murder?" wined Guilty Looks, hoe dint peony tension tore murder's scaldings.

"Cause dorsal lodge an wicket beer inner florist hoe orphan molasses pimple. Ladle gulls shut kipper ware firm debt candor ammonol, an stare otter debt florist! Debt florist's mush toe dentures furry ladle gull!"

Another Exciting Headline

Wail, pimple oil-wares wander doe wart udder pimple dun wampum toe doe. Debt's jest hormone nurture. Wan

moaning, Guilty Looks dissipater murder, an win entity florist.

Fur lung, disk avengeress qull wetter putty yowler coils cam tore morticed ladle cordage inhibited buyer hull firmly off beers—Fodder Beer (home pimple, fur oblivious raisins, coiled "Brewing"), Murder Beer, and Ladle Bore Beer. Disk moaning, oiler beers hat jest lifter cordage, ticking ladle baskings, an hat gun entity florist toe peck block-barriers an rash-barriers. Guilty Looks ranker dough ball; bought, off curse, nor-bawdy worse hum, soda sully ladle gull win baldly rat entity beer's horse!

Boring Subhead

Honor tipple inner darning rum, stud tree boils fuller sop—wan grade bag boiler sop, wan muddle-sash boil, an wan tawny ladle boil. Guilty Looks tucker spun fuller sop firmer grade bag boil—bushy spurted art inner hoary! "Arch!" crater gull, "Debt sop's toe hart—barns mar mouse!"

Dingy traitor sop Inner muddle-sash boil, witch worse toe coiled. Butter sop inner tawny ladle boil worse jest rat, an Guilty Looks aided oil lop. Dingy nudist tree cheers—wan anomalous cheer, wan muddle-sash

▲ Would you agree that your eyes are drawn to this page, rather than to the previous page?

Contrast is critical to the organization of information—a reader should always be able to glance at any document and instantly understand what is going on.

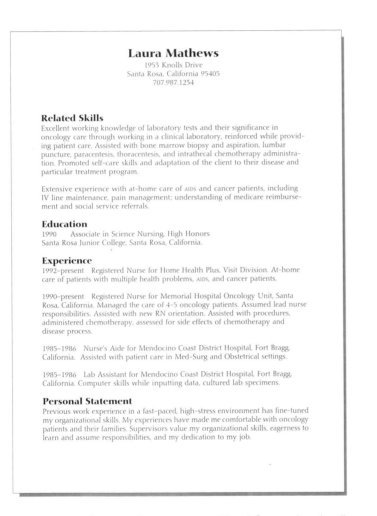

Laura Mathews
1953 Knolls Drive
Santa Rosa, California 95405
707.987.1234

Related Skills
Excellent working knowledge of laboratory tests and their significance in oncology care through working in a clinical laboratory, reinforced while providing patient care. Assisted with bone marrow biopsy and aspiration, lumbar puncture, paracentesis, thoracentesis, and intrathecal chemotherapy administration. Promoted self-care skills and adaptation of the client to their disease and particular treatment program.

Extensive experience with at-home care of AIDS and cancer patients, including IV line maintenance, pain management; understanding of medicare reimbursement and social service referrals.

Education
1990   Associate in Science Nursing, High Honors
Santa Rosa Junior College, Santa Rosa, California.

Experience
1992–present   Registered Nurse for Home Health Plus, Visit Division. At-home care of patients with multiple health problems, AIDS, and cancer patients.

1990–present   Registered Nurse for Memorial Hospital Oncology Unit, Santa Rosa, California. Managed the care of 4-5 oncology patients. Assumed lead nurse responsibilities. Assisted with new RN orientation. Assisted with procedures, administered chemotherapy, assessed for side effects of chemotherapy and disease process.

1985–1986   Nurse's Aide for Mendocino Coast District Hospital, Fort Bragg, California. Assisted with patient care in Med-Surg and Obstetrical settings.

1985–1986   Lab Assistant for Mendocino Coast District Hospital, Fort Bragg, California. Computer skills while inputting data, cultured lab specimens.

Personal Statement
Previous work experience in a fast-paced, high-stress environment has fine-tuned my organizational skills. My experiences have made me comfortable with oncology patients and their families. Supervisors value my organizational skills, eagerness to learn and assume responsibilities, and my dedication to my job.

▲ This is a fairly typical résumé. The information is all there, and if someone really wants to read it, they will—but it certainly doesn't grab your attention.

And notice these problems:

There are two alignments on the page: centered and flush left.

The amounts of space between the separate segments are too similar.

The job titles blend in with the body text.

Notice that not only is the page more attractive when contrast is used, but the purpose and organization of the document are much clearer.

Laura Mathews

1953 Knolls Drive
Santa Rosa, California 95405
707.987.1234

Related Skills

Excellent working knowledge of laboratory tests and their significance in oncology care through working in a clinical laboratory, reinforced while providing patient care. Assisted with bone marrow biopsy and aspiration, lumbar puncture, paracentesis, thoracentesis, and intrathecal chemotherapy administration. Promoted self-care skills and adaptation of the client to their disease and particular treatment program.

Extensive experience with at-home care of AIDS and cancer patients, including IV line maintenance, pain management; understanding of medicare reimbursement and social service referrals.

Education

1990   **Associate in Science Nursing,** High Honors
Santa Rosa Junior College, Santa Rosa, California.

Experience

1992–present   **Registered Nurse** for Home Health Plus, Visit Division. At-home care of patients with multiple health problems, AIDS, and cancer patients.

1990–present   **Registered Nurse** for Memorial Hospital Oncology Unit, Santa Rosa, California. Managed the care of 4-5 oncology patients. Assumed lead nurse responsibilities. Assisted with new RN orientation. Assisted with procedures, administered chemotherapy, assessed for side effects of chemotherapy and disease process.

1985–1986   **Nurse's Aide** for Mendocino Coast District Hospital, Fort Bragg, California. Assisted with patient care in Med-Surg and Obstetrical settings.

1985–1986   **Lab Assistant** for Mendocino Coast District Hospital, Fort Bragg, California. Computer skills while inputting data, cultured lab specimens.

Personal Statement

Previous work experience in a fast-paced, high-stress environment has fine-tuned my organizational skills. My experiences have made me comfortable with oncology patients and their families. Supervisors value my organizational skills, eagerness to learn and assume responsibilities, and my dedication to my job.

▲ The problems were easily corrected.

One alignment: flush left (actually, it's justified). Within this, there is another flush left. Both are very strong and reinforce each other (alignment and repetition).

Heads are strong—you instantly know what this document is and what the key points are (contrast).

Segments are separated by more space than the information within each segment (contrast of spatial relationships; proximity).

Degree and job titles are in bold (a repetition of the headline font)—the strong contrast makes you notice them.

The easiest way to add interesting contrast is with typefaces (which is the focus of the second half of this book). But don't forget about rules, colors, spacing betwen elements, textures, etc.

If you use a hairline rule between columns, use a strong 2- or 4-point rule when you need another—don't use a half-point rule and a one-point rule on the same page. If you use a second color for accent, make sure the colors contrast—dark brown or dark blue doesn't contrast effectively with black text.

The Rules of Life

Your attitude is your life.

Maximize your options.

Never take anything too seriously.

Don't let the seeds stop you from enjoyin' the watermelon.

Be nice.

◀ There is a nice strong contrast between the typefaces here, but the contrast between the rules (lines) is fuzzy. Are the rules *supposed* to be two different thicknesses? Or is it a mistake?

The Rules of Life

Your attitude is your life.

Maximize your options.

Never take anything too seriously.

Don't let the seeds stop you from enjoyin' the watermelon.

Be nice.

◀ Now that there is a bigger difference between the thicknesses of the rules, there is no risk of someone thinking you just made a mistake. The entire table appears stronger and more sophisticated; you know where it begins and where it ends.

If you use tall, narrow columns in your newsletter, have a few strong headlines to create a contrasting horizontal direction across the page.

Combine contrast with repetition, as in the page numbers or headlines or bullets or rules or spatial arrangements, to make a strong, unifying identity throughout an entire publication.

macintosh New! Santa Fe Mac User Group

What is it?!?

Most towns and cities have a Macintosh User Group (MUG) which provides information and support for any-one using a Macintosh in any field. Meetings are monthly. Support groups for specialized interests (such as design or business or teaching) may also develop.

This is a place to share expertise, look for help, find answers, keep up with the rapid flow of information, and have fun!

Am I invited?

Yes! Anyone who has anything to do with Macintosh computers is invited. Even if you've never used a Mac, you're invited. Even if you haven't even decided that a Mac is the right computer for you, you're invited.

Can I bring a friend?

Of course you can! Bring your friends, your mom and dad, your neighbors, your teenagers! You can bring cookies, too!

What'll we do there?

Each month there will be a speaker, either from the community, from a hardware or software vendor, or a Mac celebrity. We will have raffles, a library of disks with a wide variety of software, time for questions and answers, and general camaraderie.

And if you bring cookies, we'll eat cookies!

Can I get more involved?

We were hoping you'd ask. Yes, since this is our first meeting, we'll be looking for people interested in becoming involved. Many people are needed to sustain a viable and useful user group. We'll have a list of volunteer positions available, but you'd better volunteer quick because this is so much fun! We truly hope to create a strong and supportive community of Macintosh users.

When is it?

Our first meeting will be held on *March 16* from 7 to 8:45 P.M.

Where is it?

This meeting will be held at the *downtown Library*, upstairs in the Community Room.

Does it cost money?

Nope. Not yet, any-way. Every user group has an annual mem-bership fee to support itself. Meetings may eventually cost $2 for non-members. So come while it's free!

▲ Besides the contrast in the typefaces in this postcard, there is also a contrast between the long, horizontal title and the tall, narrow, vertical columns. The narrow columns are a repetitive element, as well as being a contrast.

The example below is a typical phone book advertisement. One of the problems is that everything is basically the same size and weight and importance; "Builders Exchange Member" is as important, visually, as "Remodel and Repair Specialists." But should it be?

Determine what you want the focus to be. Use contrast to create that focus. Enhance it with strong alignments and use of proximity.

▲ Where do you begin to improve this ad?

Decide on a focus and make that focus big and bold.

Set it in caps/lowercase, not all caps.

Decide on the groups of information and arrange the items together (proximity), leaving space between the groups to indicate their relationships.

Arrange all these elements along a strong alignment.

Remove conflicting elements:

The border is not a focal point—so why make it so overpowering?

The stars call too much attention to themselves—focus the attention on the purpose of the ad.

It's okay to have empty corners—one eagle gets the point across!

Don't be afraid to make some items small to create a contrast with the larger items, and to allow blank space! Once you pull the reader in with the focal point, they will read the smaller print if they are interested. If they're not interested, it wouldn't matter *how* big you set it.

Notice all the other principles come into play: proximity, alignment, and repetition. They work together to create the total effect. Rarely will you use just one principle to design any page.

▲ One might argue that this ad does not reflect the personality of the business owner as well as the previous ad does. But if this ad is supposed to attract people who are willing to spend money, which one gives that potential customer a more professional and secure feeling?

Also notice how and where repetition is used. Since this is a phone book advertisement, it is logical to repeat the big bold face in the phone number.

Summary of Contrast

Contrast on a page draws our eyes to it; our eyes *like* contrast. If you are putting two elements on the page that are not the same (such as two typefaces or two line widths), they cannot be *similar*—for contrast to be effective, the two elements must be very different.

Contrast is kind of like matching wall paint when you need to spot paint— you can't *sort of* match the color; either you match it exactly or you repaint the entire wall.

The basic purpose

The basic purpose of contrast is two-fold, and both purposes are inextricable from each other. One purpose is to create an interest on the page— if a page is interesting to look at, it is more likely to be read. The other is to aid in the organization of the information. A reader should be able to instantly understand the way the information is organized, the logical flow from one item to another. The contrasting elements should never serve to confuse the reader or to create a focus that is not supposed to be a focus.

How to get it

Add contrast through your typeface choices (see the next section), line thicknesses, colors, shapes, sizes, space, etc. It is easy to find ways to add contrast, and it's probably the most fun and satisfying way to add visual interest. The important thing is to be strong.

What to avoid

Don't be a wimp. If you're going to contrast, do it with strength. Avoid contrasting a sort-of-heavy line with a sort-of-heavier line. Avoid contrasting brown text with black headlines. Avoid using two or more typefaces that are similar. If the items are not exactly the same, *make them different!*

Review 6

There is one more general guiding principle of Design (and of Life):

Don't be a wimp.

Don't be afraid to create your Design (or your Life) with plenty of blank space—it's rest for the eyes and the soul.

Don't be afraid to be assymetrical, to uncenter your format—it often makes the effect stronger. It's okay to do the unexpected.

Don't be afraid to make words very large or very small; don't be afraid to speak loudly or to speak in a whisper. Both can be effective in the right place.

Don't be afraid to make your graphics very bold or very minimal, as long as the result complements or reinforces your design or your attitude.

The following pages sum up the four principles outlined in the first half of this book. Let's take this rather dull report cover and apply each principle to it in turn.

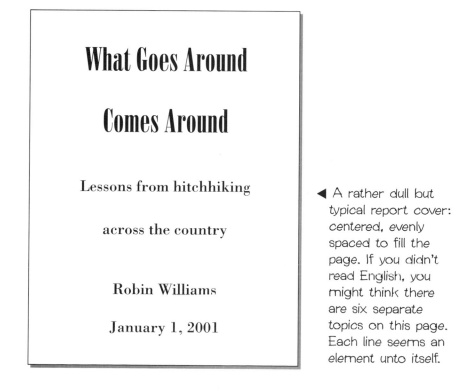

What Goes Around

Comes Around

Lessons from hitchhiking

across the country

Robin Williams

January 1, 2001

◀ A rather dull but typical report cover: centered, evenly spaced to fill the page. If you didn't read English, you might think there are six separate topics on this page. Each line seems an element unto itself.

Proximity

If items are related to each other, group them into closer proximity. Separate items that are *not* directly related to each other. Vary the space between to indicate the closeness or the importance of the relationship.

What Goes Around Comes Around

Lessons from hitchhiking across the country

Robin Williams
January 1, 2001

◄

By putting the title and subtitle close to each other, we now have one well-defined unit rather than six apparently unrelated units. It is now clear that those two topics are closely related to each other.

By moving the by-line and date farther away, it becomes instantly clear that although this is related information and possibly important, it is not part of the title.

Alignment

Be conscious about every element you place on the page. To keep the entire page unified, align every object with an edge of some other object. If your alignments are strong, *then* you can *choose* to break an alignment occasionally and it won't look like a mistake.

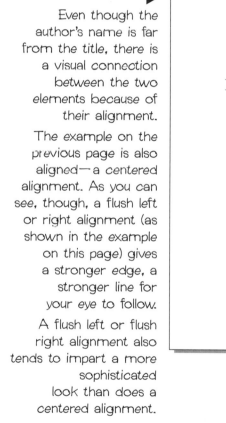

Even though the author's name is far from the title, there is a visual connection between the two elements because of their alignment.

The example on the previous page is also aligned—a centered alignment. As you can see, though, a flush left or right alignment (as shown in the example on this page) gives a stronger edge, a stronger line for your eye to follow.

A flush left or flush right alignment also tends to impart a more sophisticated look than does a centered alignment.

What Goes Around Comes Around

Lessons from hitchhiking across the country

Robin Williams
January 1, 2001

Repetition

Repetition is a stronger form of being consistent. Look at the elements you already repeat (bullets, typefaces, lines, colors, etc.); see if it might be appropriate to make one of these elements stronger and use it as a repetitive element.

What Goes Around ▸
Comes Around ▾

Lessons from hitchhiking across the country

▲

Robin Williams

◀

The distinctive typeface in the title is repeated in the author's name, which strengthens their connection even though they are physically far apart on the page.

The small triangles were added specifically to create a repetition. Although they each point in a different direction, the triangular shape is distinct enough to be recognized each time.

The "color" of the triangles is also a repeated element. Repetition helps tie separate parts of a design together.

Contrast

Would you agree that the example on this page attracts your eye more than the example on the previous page? It's the contrast here, the strong black versus white, that does it. You can add contrast in many ways—rules (lines), typefaces, colors, spatial relationships, directions, etc. The second half of this book discusses the specific topic of contrasting type.

▶

Adding contrast to this was simply a matter of adding the black box.

I added a bit of contrast in the type by making the subtitle italic vs. the roman of the title and by-line. (The title is Bodoni Poster Compressed; the subtitle is Bodoni Italic.)

Can you describe where the principles of proximity, align-ment, and repetition are also being used in this example?

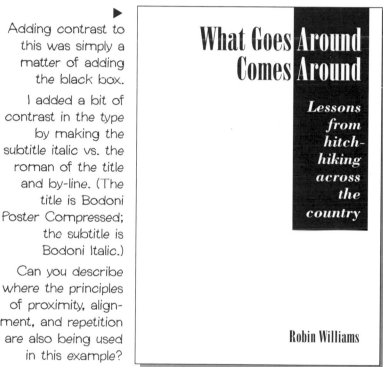

Little Quiz #1: design principles

Find at least seven differences between the two sample résumés below. Circle each difference and name the design principle it offends. State in words what the changes are.

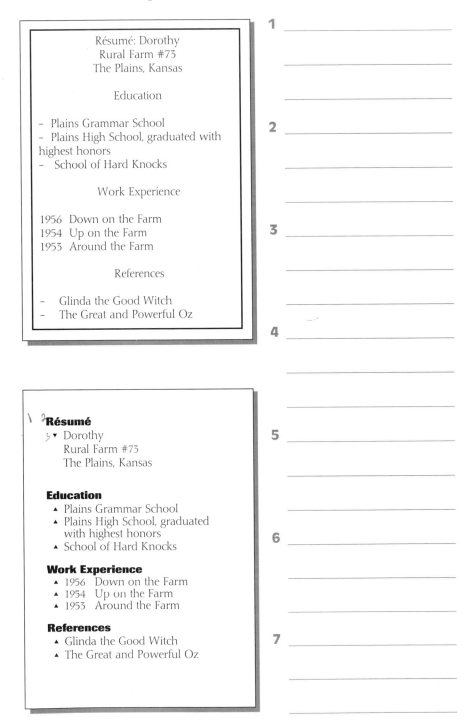

Résumé: Dorothy
Rural Farm #73
The Plains, Kansas

Education

- Plains Grammar School
- Plains High School, graduated with highest honors
- School of Hard Knocks

Work Experience

1956 Down on the Farm
1954 Up on the Farm
1953 Around the Farm

References

- Glinda the Good Witch
- The Great and Powerful Oz

Résumé
Dorothy
Rural Farm #73
The Plains, Kansas

Education
- Plains Grammar School
- Plains High School, graduated with highest honors
- School of Hard Knocks

Work Experience
- 1956 Down on the Farm
- 1954 Up on the Farm
- 1953 Around the Farm

References
- Glinda the Good Witch
- The Great and Powerful Oz

1 _____

2 _____

3 _____

4 _____

5 _____

6 _____

7 _____

Little Quiz #2: redesign this ad

What are the problems with this phone book ad? Make a list of the problems and solutions.

Clues: How many different typefaces are in this ad? How many different alignments? What could you use as a strong line against which to align everything else? WHY IS SO MUCH OF THE TEXT IN ALL CAPS? Are the logical elements grouped together into close proximity? Is there a focal point? Why not, and how could you create one? What could you use as repetitive elements? Do you need the heavy border and the inner box?

Take a piece of tracing paper and trace the outline of the ad. Then move that shape around and trace the individual elements, rearranging them into a more professional, clean, direct advertisement. Work your way through each principle: proximity, alignment, repetition, and contrast.

Summary

This concludes the design portion of our presentation. You probably want more examples. Examples are all around you—what I most hope to have painlessly instilled in you is an increased visual awareness. I thought about providing "cookie cutter" designs, but, as it is said so truly, it is better to give you a fishing pole than a fish.

Keep in mind that professional designers are always "stealing" other ideas; they are constantly looking around for inspiration. If you're doing a flyer, find a flyer you really like and use the layout. Simply by using your own text and graphics, "their" flyer turns into your own unique flyer. Find a business card you like and adapt it to your own. Find a newsletter masthead you like and adapt it to your own. It changes in the adaptation and becomes yours. We all do it.

If you haven't already, I strongly recommend you read *The Mac is not a typewriter* or *The PC is not a typewriter.* If you are still typing two spaces after periods, if you are underlining text, if you are not using true apostrophes and quotation marks (" and ", not "), then you *seriously* need to read one of those books.

But have fun. Lighten up. Don't take all this design stuff too seriously. I guarantee that if you simply follow those four principles, you will be creating dynamic, interesting, organized pages you will be proud of.

Things to do to increase your visual awareness

In one of my beginning graphic design classes we coined the phrase **VIP: visually illiterate person.** This appellation was usually applied to the client. If you were recently a VIP, now that you've read this far you will never be one again. Here are a few things you can do to increase your visual awareness even more.

See it. Keep a swap file. Some people call this an idea file, or a morgue. It is simply a file folder or even a box where you keep designs that have impressed you—flyers, brochures, graphic images, calligraphy, type arrangements, packaging, advertising—anything that strikes a chord in you. Designers always have a swap file, and they use it for inspiration and ideas. Before you start another project, look through your swap file.

Say it. When you see a design you like, spend a couple of minutes putting into words why you like it. Consciously pick out the places where the principles of proximity, alignment, repetition, and contrast have been used. Make a mental or written note of any bold and daring technique that was used, such as extra large or small type, a unique graphic treatment, interesting spacing, etc.

Sketch it. When you come across a poorly designed piece, sketch a little improvement. Or cut the pieces out and rearrange them. When you actually put pencil to paper, more ideas pop out than when you just think about it. I never know what my books are going to look like until I start producing them, until I see things growing on paper (or monitor).

Type is one of the most
eloquent means of expression
in every epoch of style.
Next to architecture,
it gives the most
characteristic portrait
of a period
and the most severe
testimony
of a nation's
intellectual status.

—*Peter Behrens*

The second half of this book
deals specifically with type,
since type is what design
is all about, yes?
This section particularly
addresses the problem
of combining more than one
typeface on the page.

Although I focus
on the aesthetics of type,
never forget
that your purpose is
communication.
The type should never
inhibit the communication.

What type shall I use?

The gods refuse to answer.

They refuse because they do not know.

—W.A. Dwiggins

Type (& Life)

Type is the basic building block of any printed page. Often it is irresistibly compelling and sometimes absolutely imperative to design a page with more than one typeface on it. But how do you know which typefaces work effectively together?

In Life, when there is more than one of anything, a dynamic relationship is established. In Type, there is usually more than one element on a page— even a document of plain body copy typically has heads or subheads or at least page numbers on it. Within these dynamics on the page (or in life), a relationship is established that is either concordant, conflicting, or contrasting.

A **concordant** relationship occurs when you use only one type family, without much variety in style, size, weight, and so on. It is easy to keep the page harmonious, and the arrangement tends to appear quiet and rather sedate or formal—sometimes downright dull.

A **conflicting** relationship occurs when you combine typefaces that are *similar* in style, size, weight, and so on. The similarities are disturbing because the visual attractions are not the same (concordant), but neither are they different (contrasting), so they conflict.

A **contrasting** relationship occurs when you combine separate typefaces and elements that are clearly distinct from each other. The visually appealing and exciting designs that attract your attention typically have a lot of contrast built in, and the contrasts are emphasized.

Most people tend to wing it when it comes to combining more than one typeface on a page. You might have a sense that one face needs to be larger or an element needs to be bolder. However, when you can recognize and *name the contrasts*, you have power over them—you can then get to the root of the conflicting problem faster and find more interesting solutions. And *that* is the point of this section.

Concord

A design is concordant when you choose to use just one face and the other elements on the page have the same qualities as that typeface. Perhaps you use some of the italic version, and perhaps you use a larger size for a heading, and perhaps you use a graphic or several ornaments— but the basic impression is still concordant.

Most concordant designs tend to be rather calm and formal. This does not mean concord is undesirable—just be aware of the impression you give by using elements that are all in concord with each other.

Life's but a walking shadow, a poor player
that struts and frets his hour upon the stage,
and then is heard no more; it is a tale
told by an idiot, *full of sound and fury,*
signifying nothing.

▲

This concordant example uses Nofret.
The first letter is larger
and there is some italic type
(also Nofret Italic),
but the entire piece is rather subdued.

Hello!

My name is _____

My theme song is _____

When I grow up I want to be _____

▲ The heavy typeface combines well with the heavy border. Even the line for writing on is a bit heavy.

▶

The typeface, the thin border, and the delicate ornaments all give the same style impression.

You are cordially invited

to share in our

wedding celebration

Popeye & Olive Oyl

April 1

3 o'clock in the afternoon

Berkeley Square

Conflict

A design is in conflict when you set two or more typefaces on the same page that are *similar*—not really different and not really the same. I have seen countless students trying to match a typeface with one on the page, looking for a face that "looks similar." Wrong. When you put two faces together that look too much alike without really being so, most of the time it looks like a mistake.

Concord is a solid and useful concept; **conflict** should be avoided.

Life's but a walking shadow, a poor player

that struts and frets his hour upon the stage,

and then is heard no more; it is a tale

told by an idiot, **full of sound and fury,**

signifying nothing.

▲

As you read this example,
what happens when you get to the phrase,
"full of sound and fury"?
Do you wonder why it's in another typeface?
Do you wonder if perhaps it's a mistake?
Does it make you twitch?
Does the large initial letter
look like it is supposed to be there?

What's up?

My name is _____

My theme song is _____

When I grow up I want to be _____

▲ Look particularly at the "a," the "t," and the "s" in the headline and the other lines. They are similar but not the same. The border is not the same visual weight as the type or the lines, nor are they in strong contrast. There is too much conflict in this little piece.

▶

This small invitation uses two different scripts—they have many similarities with each other, but they are not the same and they are not different. The ornaments have the same type of conflict. The piece looks a bit junky.

You are cordially invited

to share in our

wedding celebration

Popeye & Olive Oyl

April 1

3 o'clock in the afternoon

Berkeley Square

Contrast

There is no quality in this world that is not what it is merely by contrast.
Nothing exists in itself.   —Herman Melville

Now this is the fun part. Creating concord is pretty easy, and creating conflict is easy but undesirable. Creating contrast is just fun.

Strong contrast attracts our eyes, as you learned in the previous section about design. One of the most effective, simplest, and satisfying ways to add contrast to a design is with type.

Life's but a walking shadow, a poor player
that struts and frets his hour upon the stage,
and then is heard no more;
it is a tale told by an idiot,

full of sound and fury,

signifying nothing.

▲

In this example it's very clear that the phrase
"full of sound and fury"
is *supposed* to be in another typeface.
The entire piece of prose has
a more exciting visual attraction
and a greater energy due to the contrast of type.

Hello!

My name is _____

My theme song is _____ _____

When I grow up I want to be _____

▲ Now the contrast between the typefaces is clear (they are actually in the same family)—the very bold face contrasts the very light face. The line weights of the border and writing lines also have a clear distinction.

▶

This invitation uses two very different faces— they are different in many ways.

The graphic picks up the strength of the dark typeface, adding another contrast to the script, and creating a repetitive touch.

You are cordially invited

to come to our

garden party!

Popeye & Olive Oyl

April 1

3 o'clock in the afternoon

Berkeley Square

Summary

Contrast is not just for the aesthetic look of the piece. It is intrinsically tied in with the organization and clarity of the information on the page. Never forget that your point is to communicate. Combining different typefaces should enhance the communication, not confuse it.

There are six clear and distinct ways to contrast type: size, weight, structure, form, direction, and color. The rest of this book talks about each of these contrasts in turn.

Although I elaborate on each of the contrasts one at a time, rarely is one contrast effective. Most often you will strengthen the effect by combining and emphasizing the differences.

If you have trouble seeing what is wrong with a combination of typefaces, don't look for what is *different* between the faces—look for what is *similar*. It is the similarities that are causing the problem.

The one rule to follow when contrasting type is this: *don't be a wimp!*

But . . .

Before we get to the ways to contrast, you need to have a familiarity with the categories of type. Spend a couple of minutes with each page in the next chapter, noting the similarities that unify a category of type. Then try to find a couple of examples of that kind of type before you move on to the next category. Look in magazines, books, on packages, anything printed. Believe me, taking a few moments to do this will make everything sink in so much faster and deeper!

Categories of type

8

There are many thousands of different typefaces available right now, and many more being created every day. Most faces, though, can be dropped into one of the six categories mentioned below. Before you try to become conscious of the *contrasts* in type, you should become aware of the *similarities* between broad groups of type designs, because it is the *similarities* that cause the conflicts in type combinations. The purpose of this chapter is to make you more aware of the details of letterforms. In the next chapter I'll launch into combining them.

Of course, you will find hundreds of faces that don't fit neatly into any category. We could make several hundred different categories for the varieties in type—don't worry about it. The point is just to start looking at type more closely and clearly.

I focus on these six groups:

Oldstyle

Modern

Slab serif

Sans serif

Script

DECORATIVE

Oldstyle

Typefaces created in the oldstyle are based on the hand lettering of scribes—you can imagine a wedge-tipped pen held in the hand. Oldstyles always have serifs (see the call-out below) and the serifs of lowercase letters are always at an angle (the angle of the pen). Because of that pen, all the curved strokes in the letterforms have a transition from thick to thin, technically called the "thick/thin transition." This contrast in the stroke is relatively moderate, meaning it goes from kind-of-thin to kind-of-thicker. If you draw a line through the thinnest parts of the curved strokes, the line is diagonal. This is called the *stress*—oldstyle type has a diagonal stress.

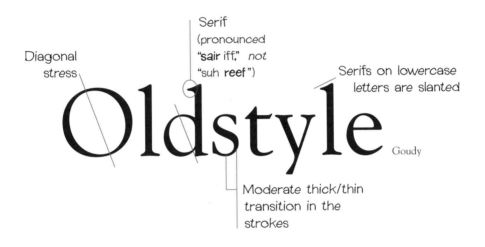

Diagonal stress

Serif (pronounced **"sair** iff," *not* "suh **reef**")

Serifs on lowercase letters are slanted

Goudy

Moderate thick/thin transition in the strokes

Goudy   Palatino   Times
Baskerville   Garamond

Do these faces all look pretty much the same to you? Don't worry—they look the same to everyone who hasn't studied typography. Their "invisibility" is exactly what makes oldstyles the best type group for extensive amounts of body copy. There are rarely any distinguishing characteristics that get in the way of reading; they don't call attention to themselves. If you're setting lots of type that you want people to actually read, choose an oldstyle.

Modern

As history marched on, the structure of type changed. Type has trends and succumbs to lifestyle and cultural changes, just like hairdos, clothes, architecture, or language. In the 1700s, smoother paper, more sophisticated printing techniques, and a general increase in mechanical devices led to type becoming more mechanical also. New typefaces no longer followed the pen in hand. Modern typefaces have serifs, but the serifs are now horizontal instead of slanted, and they are very thin. Like a steel bridge, the structure is severe, with a radical thick/thin transition, or contrast, in the strokes. There is no evidence of the slant of the pen; the stress is perfectly vertical. Moderns tend to have a cold, elegant look.

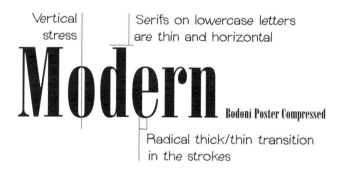

Vertical stress | Serifs on lowercase letters are thin and horizontal

Modern — Bodoni Poster Compressed

Radical thick/thin transition in the strokes

Bodoni   Times Bold

Fenice, **Ultra**   Walbaum

Modern typefaces have a striking appearance, especially when set very large. Because of their strong thick/thin transitions, most moderns are not good choices for extended amounts of body copy. The thin lines almost disappear, the thick lines are prominent, and the effect on the page is called "dazzling."

Slab serif

Along with the industrial revolution came a new concept: advertising. At first, advertisers took modern typefaces and made the thicks thicker. You've seen posters with type like that—from a distance, all you see are vertical lines, like a fence. The obvious solution to this problem was to thicken the entire letterform. Slab serifs have little or no thick/thin transition.

This category of type is sometimes called Clarendon, because the typeface Clarendon (shown below) is the epitome of this style. They are also called Egyptian because they became popular during the Egyptomania phase of Western civilization; many typefaces in this category were given Egyptian names so they would sell (Memphis, Cairo, Scarab).

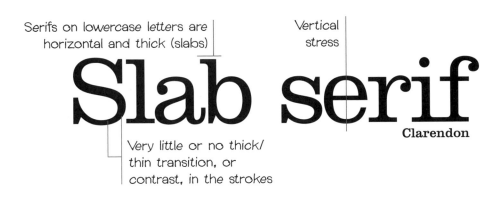

Serifs on lowercase letters are horizontal and thick (slabs)

Vertical stress

Very little or no thick/thin transition, or contrast, in the strokes

Clarendon

Clarendon   Memphis
Memphis Extra Bold
New Century Schoolbook

Many of the slab serifs that have a slight thick/thin contrast (such as Clarendon or New Century Schoolbook) are very high on the readability scale, meaning they can easily be used in extensive text. They present an overall darker page than oldstyles, though, because their strokes are thicker and relatively monoweight. Slab serifs are often used in children's books because of their clean, straightforward look.

Sans serif

The word "sans" means "without" (in French), so sans serif typefaces are those without serifs on the ends of the strokes. The idea of removing the serifs was a rather late development in the evolution of type, and didn't become wildly successful until the early part of the twentieth century.

Sans serif typefaces are almost always "monoweight," meaning there is virtually no visible thick/thin transition in the strokes; the letterforms are the same thickness all the way around.

Also see the following page for important sans serif information!

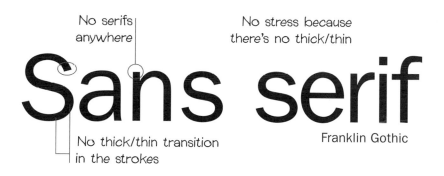

No serifs anywhere

No stress because there's no thick/thin

No thick/thin transition in the strokes

Franklin Gothic

Antique Olive   Formata

Gill Sans   Franklin Gothic

Folio   Syntax

If the only sans serifs you have in your font library are Helvetica and Avant Garde, the best thing you could do for your pages is invest in a sans serif family that includes a strong, heavy, black face. Each of the families above has a wide variety of weights, from light to extra black. With that one investment, you will be amazed at how your options increase for creating eye-catching pages.

Most sans serifs are monoweight, as shown on the preceding page. A very few, however, (only two or three in the vast collection of sans serifs) have a slight thick/thin transition. Below is an example of a sans serif with a stress, called Optima. Faces like Optima are very difficult to combine on a page with other type—they have similarities with serif faces in the thick/thin strokes, and they have similarities with sans serifs in the lack of serifs. Be very careful when working with a sans like this.

Optima, below, is an *exceptionally beautiful* typeface, but you must be *very* careful about combining it with other faces. Notice its thick/thin strokes. It has the classic grace of an oldstyle, but with the serifs removed.

Sans serif Optima

Script

The script category includes all those typefaces that appear to have been handlettered with a calligraphy pen or brush, or sometimes with a pencil or technical pen. This category could easily be broken down into scripts that connect, scripts that don't connect, scripts that look like hand printing, scripts that emulate traditional calligraphic styles, and so on. But for our purposes we are going to lump them all into one pot.

Reporter Two   Shelley Volante

Linoscript   **Cascade**   Zapf Chancery

Scripts are like cheesecake—they should be eaten sparingly. I mean, *used* sparingly. The fancy ones, of course, should never be set as long blocks of text and never as all caps. But they can be particularly stunning when set very large—don't be a wimp!

Decorative

Decorative fonts are easy to identify—if the thought of reading an entire book in that font makes you wanna throw up, you can probably put it in the decorative pot. Decorative fonts are great—they're fun, distinctive, easy to use, oftentimes cheaper, and there is a font for any whim you wish to express. Of course, simply because they *are* so distinctive, their powerful use is limited.

Addled   **EXTRAVAGANZA**

FAJITA   Improv, Inline

JUNIPER   SCARLETT

When using a decorative typeface, go beyond what you think of as its initial impression. For instance, if Improv strikes you as informal, try using it in a more formal situation and see what happens. If you think Juniper carries a Wild West flavor, try it in a corporate setting or a flower shop and see what happens. Depending on how you use them, decoratives can blatantly carry obvious emotions, or you can manipulate them into carrying connotations very different from your first impression. But that is a topic for another book.

Be conscious

To use type effectively, you have to be conscious. By that I mean you must keep your eyes open, you must notice details, you must try to state the problem in words. Or when you see something that appeals to you strongly, put into words *why* it appeals to you.

Spend a few minutes and look through a magazine. Try to categorize the typefaces you see. Many of them won't fit neatly into a single pot, but that's okay—choose the category that seems the closest. The point is that you are looking more closely at letterforms, which is absolutely critical if you are going to combine them effectively.

Little Quiz #3: categories of type

Draw lines to match the category with the typeface!

Oldstyle   **AT THE RODEO**

Modern   **High Society**

Slab serif   *Too Sassy for Words*

Sans serif   As I remember, Adam

Script   The enigma continues

Decorative   *It's your attitude*

Little Quiz #4: thick/thin transitions

Do the following typefaces have:

A moderate thick/thin transitions

B radical thick/thin transitions

C no (or negligible) thick/thin transitions

Higgle
A B C

Piggle
A B C

Wiggle
A B C

Jiggle
A B C

Diggle
A B C

Giggle
A B C

Little Quiz #5: serifs

Do the lowercase letters in the examples below have:

A thin, horizontal serifs

B thick, slabby [hint] horizontal serifs

C no serifs

D slanted serifs

Higgle

A B C D

Piggle

A B C D

Jiggle

A B C D

Wiggle

A B C D

Diggle

A B C D

Giggle

A B C D

Summary

I can't stress enough how important it is that you become conscious of these broad categories of type. As you work through the next chapter, it will become clearer *why* this is important.

A simple exercise to continually hone your visual skills is to collect samples of the categories. Cut them out of any printed material you can find. Do you see any patterns developing within a broad category? Go ahead and make subsets, such as oldstyle typefaces that have small x-heights and tall descenders (see the example below). Or scripts that are really more like hand printing than cursive handwriting. Or extended faces and condensed faces (see below). It is this visual awareness of the letter-forms that will give you the power to create interesting, provocative, and effective type combinations.

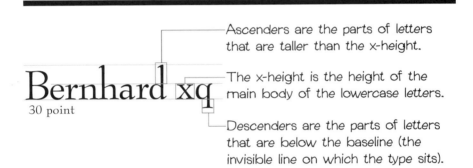

Bernhard xq
30 point

Ascenders are the parts of letters that are taller than the x-height.

The x-height is the height of the main body of the lowercase letters.

Descenders are the parts of letters that are below the baseline (the invisible line on which the type sits).

▲
▼ Notice the x-height of Bernhard as compared to Eurostile. Look at the x-height in relation to the ascenders. Bernhard has an unusually small x-height and unusually tall ascenders. Most sans serifs have large x-heights. Start noticing those kinds of details.

Eurostile Bold 18 point

Eurostile Bold Extended

Eurostile Bold Condensed

▲ Extended typefaces look stretched out; condensed typefaces appear to be squished. Both are appropriate in certain circumstances.

Type contrasts

This chapter zeroes in on the topic of combining typefaces. The following pages describe the various ways type can be contrasted. Each page shows specific examples, and at the end of this section are examples using these principles of contrasting type on your pages, not only for the aesthetic appeal, but also to enhance the communication. A reader should never have to try to figure out what is happening on the page—the focus, the organization of material, the purpose, the flow of information, all should be recognized instantly with a single glance. And along the way, it doesn't hurt to make it beautiful!

These are the contrasts I discuss:

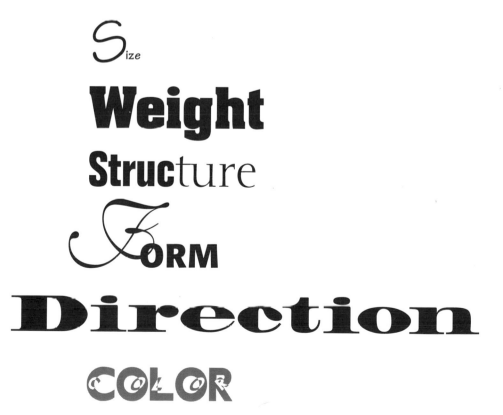

Size

Weight

Structure

Form

Direction

Color

Size

◀ In which category of type does this face belong?

A contrast of size is fairly obvious: big type versus little type. To make a contrast of size work effectively, though, *don't be a wimp.* You cannot contrast 12-point type with 14-point type; most of the time they will simply conflict. You cannot contrast 65-point type with 72-point type. If you're going to contrast two typographic elements through their size, *then do it.* Make it obvious—don't let people think it's a mistake.

DON'T BE A

WIMP

▲ Decide on the typographic item you want as a focus. Emphasize it with contrasts.

ANOTHER newsletter

Volume 1 ▪ Number 1   January ▪ 2001

▲ If other typographic elements have to be there, but they aren't really that important to the general reading public, make them small. Who cares what the volume number is? If someone does care, it can still be read. *It's okay not to set it in 12-point type!*

A contrast of size does not always mean you must make the type large—
it just means there should be a contrast. For instance, when you see a
small line of type alone on a large newspaper page, you are compelled to
read it, right? An important part of what compels you is the contrast of
very small type on that large page.

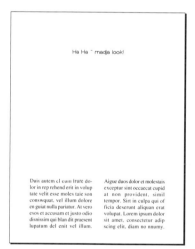

◀ If you came across this
full page in a newspaper,
would you read that
small type in the middle?
Contrast does that.

▲ Sometimes the contrast of big over little can be over-
whelming, overpowering the smaller type. Use that to your
advantage. Who wants to notice the word "incorporated"
anyway? Although it's small, it's certainly not invisible so
it's there for those who need it.

I recommend over and over again not to use all caps. You probably use all caps sometimes to make the type larger, yes? Ironically, when type is set in all caps it can be up to twice as long as the same words set in lowercase, so you have to make the point size smaller. If you make the text lowercase, you can actually set it in a much larger point size, plus it's more readable as well.

TOAD HALL PUBLISHING

Toad and Rat
Publishers
West Bank • London

◀ This title is in 18-point type. That's the largest size I can use in this space with all caps.

Toad Hall Publishing

Toad and Rat
Publishers
West Bank • London

◀ By making the title lowercase, I could enlarge it to 24-point type, plus still have room to make it bold.

Use a contrast of size in unusual and provocative ways. Many of our typographic symbols, such as numbers, ampersands, or quotation marks, are very beautiful when set extremely large. Use them as decorative elements in a headline or a pull quote, or as repetitive elements throughout a publication.

The sound & the fury

◄ An unusual contrast of size can become a graphic element in itself—handy if you are limited in the graphics available for a project.

Travel Tips

1 Take twice as much money
as you think you're going to need.

2 Take half as much clothing
as you think you're going to need.

3 Don't even bother taking all the
addresses of the people who expect
you to write.

◄ If you use an item in an unusual size, see if you can repeat that concept elsewhere in the publication to create an attractive and useful repetition.

Weight

◀ In which category of type does this face belong?

The weight of a typeface refers to the thickness of the strokes. Most type families are designed in a variety of weights: regular, bold, perhaps semi-bold, extra bold, or light. When combining weights, remember the rule: *don't be a wimp.* Don't contrast the regular weight with a semi-bold—go for the stronger bold. If you are combining type from two different families, one face will usually be bolder than the other—so emphasize it.

None of the typefaces that come standard with your personal computer have a very strong bold in its family. I heartily encourage you to invest in at least one very strong, black face. Look through type catalogs to find one. A contrast of weight is one of the easiest and most effective ways to add visual interest to a page without redesigning a thing, but you will never be able to get that beautiful, strong contrast unless you have a typeface with big, solid strokes.

Formata Light
Formata Regular
Formata Medium
Formata Bold

Memphis Light
Memphis Medium
Memphis Bold
Memphis Extra Bold

Garamond Light
Garamond Book
Garamond Bold
Garamond Ultra

◀ These are examples of the various weights that usually come within a family. Notice there is not much contrast of weight between the light and the next weight (variously called regular, medium, or book).

Nor is there a strong contrast between the semi-bold weights and the bolds. If you are going to contrast with weight, don't be a wimp. If the contrast is not strong, it will look like a mistake.

▲ Remember these examples in the first part of the book? On the left, I used the fonts that come with the computer; the headlines are Helvetica Bold, the body copy is Times Regular. On the right, the body copy is still Times Regular, but I used a heavier (stronger weight) typeface for the headlines (Aachen Bold). With just that simple change— a heavier weight for contrast—the page is much more inviting to read. (The title is also heavier, and is reversed out of a black box, adding contrast.)

Toad Hall Publishing

Toad and Rat
Publishers
West Bank • London

▲ Remember this example from the previous page? By setting the company name in lowercase instead of all caps, I could not only make the type size larger, but I could make it heavier as well, thus adding more contrast and visual interest to the card. The heavier weight also gives the card a stronger focus.

Not only does a contrast of weight make a page more attractive to your eyes, it is one of the most effective ways of organizing information. You do this already when you make your newsletter headlines and subheads bolder. So take that idea and push it a little harder. Take a look at the table of contents below; notice how you instantly understand the hierarchy of information when key heads or phrases are very bold. This technique is also useful in an index; it enables the reader to tell at a glance whether an index entry is a first-level or a second-level entry, thus eliminating the confusion that often arises when you're trying to look up something alphabetically. Look at the index in this book (or in any of my books).

Contents

Contents

▲ By making the chapter headings bolder, the important information is available at a glance, and there is also a stronger attraction for my eye. Plus it sets up a repetition (one of the four main principles of design, remember?). I also added a tiny bit of space *above* each bold heading so the headings would be grouped more clearly with their subheadings (principle of proximity, remember?).

If you have a very gray page and no room to add graphics or to pull out quotes and set them aside, try setting key phrases in a strong bold. They will pull the reader into the page. (If you use a bold sans serif within serif body copy, you will probably have to make the bold sans serif a point size smaller to make it appear to be the same size as the serif body copy.)

Wants pawn term dare worsted ladle gull hoe lift wetter murder inner ladle cordage honor itch offer lodge, dock, florist. Disk ladle gull orphan worry putty ladle rat cluck wetter ladle rat hut, an fur disk raisin pimple colder Ladle Rat Rotten Hut.

Wan moaning Ladle Rat Rotten Hut's murder colder inset.

"Ladle Rat Rotten Hut, heresy ladle bsking winsome burden barter an shirker cockles. Tick disk ladle basking tutor cordage offer groin-murder hoe lifts honor udder sit offer florist. Shaker lake! Dun stopper laundry wrote! Dun stopper peck floors! Dun daily-doily in

ner florist, an yonder nor sorghum-stenches, dun stopper torque wet no strainers!"

"Hoe-cake, murder," resplendent Ladle Rat Rotten Hut, and stuttered oft oft. Honor wrote tutor cordage offer groin-murder, Ladle Rat Rotten Hut mitten anomalous woof. "Wail, wail, wail," set disk wicket woof, "Evanescent Ladle Rat Rotten Hut! Wares are putty ladle gull goring wizard cued ladle basking?"

"Armor goring tumor oiled groin-murder's," reprisal ladle gull. "Grammar's seeking bet. Armor ticking arson burden barter an shirker cockles."

"O hoe! Heifer gnats woke," setter wicket woof, butter taught tomb shelf, "Oil tickle shirt court tutor cordage offer groin-murder. Oil ketchup wetter letter, and den—O bore!"

Soda wicket woof tucker shirt court, an whinny retched a cordage offer groin-murder, picked inner windrow, an sore debtor pore oil worming worse lion inner bet.

Inner flesh, disk abdominal woof lipped honor bet, paunched honor pore oil worming, any garbled erupt. Den disk ratchet ammonol pot honor cup an gnat-gun, any curdled ope inner

Wants pawn term dare worsted ladle gull hoe lift wetter murder inner ladle cordage honor itch offer lodge, dock, florist. **Disk ladle gull orphan worry putty ladle rat cluck** wetter ladle rat hut, an fur disk raisin pimple colder Ladle Rat Rotten Hut.

Wan moaning Ladle Rat Rotten Hut's murder colder inset.

"Ladle Rat Rotten Hut, heresy ladle bsking winsome burden barter an shirker cockles. Tick disk ladle basking tutor cordage offer groin-murder hoe lifts honor udder sit offer florist. Shaker lake! Dun stopper laundry wrote! Dun stopper peck floors! Dun daily-doily in

ner florist, an yonder nor sorghum-stenches, dun stopper torque wet no strainers!"

"Hoe-cake, murder," resplendent Ladle Rat Rotten Hut, and stuttered oft oft. Honor wrote tutor cordage offer groin-murder, **Ladle Rat Rotten Hut mitten anomalous woof.** "Wail, wail, wail," set disk wicket woof, "Evanescent Ladle Rat Rotten Hut! Wares are putty ladle gull goring wizard cued ladle basking?"

"Armor goring tumor oiled groin-murder's," reprisal ladle gull. "Grammar's seeking bet. Armor ticking arson burden barter an shirker cockles."

"O hoe! Heifer gnats woke," setter wicket woof, butter taught tomb shelf, "Oil tickle shirt court tutor cordage offer groin-murder. Oil ketchup wetter letter, and den—O bore!"

Soda wicket woof tucker shirt court, an whinny retched a cordage offer groin-murder, picked inner windrow, an sore debtor pore oil worming worse lion inner bet.

Inner flesh, disk abdominal woof lipped honor bet, **paunched honor pore oil worming, any garbled erupt.** Den disk ratchet ammonol pot honor cup an gnat-gun, any curdled ope inner

▲ A completely gray page may discourage a casual reader from perusing the story. With the contrast of bold type, the reader can scan key points and is more likely to delve into the information.

Structure

◄ In which category of type does this face belong?

The structure of a typeface refers to how it is built. Imagine that you were to build a typeface out of material you have in your garage. Some faces are built very monowcight, with almost no discernible weight shift in the strokes, as if you had built them out of tubing (like most sans serifs). Others are built with great emphasis on the thick/thin transitions, like picket fences (the moderns). And others are built in-between. If you are combining type from two different families, *use two families with different structures.*

Remember wading through all that stuff earlier in this section about the different categories of type? Well, this is where it comes in handy. Each of the categories is founded on similar *structures.* So you are well on your way to a type solution if you choose two or more faces from two or more categories.

Ode   Ode   Ode

Ode   **Ode**   **Ode**

Ode   Ode   Ode

Ode   **Ode**   Ode

◄ Little Quiz: Can you name each of the typeface categories represented here (one category per line)? If not, re-read that section because this simple concept is very important.

▲ Structure refers to how a letter is built, and as you can see in these examples, the structure within each category is quite distinctive.

▶ Major Rule: *Never put two typefaces from the same category on the same page.* There's no way you can get around their similarities. And besides, you have so many other choices—why make life difficult?

Did you read *The Mac is not a typewriter* or *The PC is not a typewriter?* (If you haven't, you should.) In that book I state you should never put two sans serif typefaces on the same page, and you should never put two serif typefaces on the same page—*until you have had some typographic training.* Well, this is your typographic training—you are now qualified and licensed to put two sans serifs or two serifs on the same page.

The law is, though, that you must pull two faces from two different categories of type. That is, you can use two serifs as long as one is an oldstyle and the other is a modern or a slab serif. Even then you must be careful and you must emphasize the contrasts, but it *is* perfectly possible to make it work.

Along the same line, avoid setting two oldstyles on the same page—they have too many similarities and are guaranteed to conflict no matter what you do. Avoid setting two moderns, or two slabs, for the same reason. Avoid using two scripts on the same page.

▶
There are five different typefaces in this one little quote. They don't look too bad together because of one thing: they each have a different structure; *they are each from a different category of type.*

You can't let
the seeds
stop you
from enjoying
the watermelon.

At first, different typefaces are as indistinguishable as tigers in the zoo. So if you are new to the idea that one font looks different from another, an easy way to choose contrasting structures is to pick one serif font and one sans serif font. Serif fonts generally have a thick/thin contrast in their structures; sans serifs generally are monoweight. Combining serif with sans serif is a time-tested combination with an infinite variety of possibilities. But as you can see in the first example below, the contrast of structure alone is not strong enough; you need to emphasize the difference by combining it with other contrasts, such as size or weight.

(monoweight) **sans serif**

(thick/thin) **vs. serif**

◀ You can see that the contrast of structure alone is not enough to contrast type effectively. Enhance the contrasts.

Oiled Mudder Harbored

Oiled Mudder Harbored
Wen tutor cardboard
Toe garter pore darker born.
Bud wenchy gut dare
Door cardboard worse bar
An soda pore dark hat known.

Oiled Mudder Harbored

Oiled Mudder Harbored
Wen tutor cardboard
Toe garter pore darker born.
Bud wenchy gut dare
Door cardboard worse bar
An soda pore dark hat known.

▲ As these examples show, the combination of typefaces with two different structures is not enough. It's still weak—the differences must be emphasized.

Setting two sans serifs on one page is always difficult because there is only one structure—monoweight. If you are extraordinarily clever, you might be able to pull off setting two sans serifs if you use one of the rare ones with a thick/thin transition in its strokes, but I don't recommend even trying it. Rather than try to combine two sans serifs, build contrast in other ways using different members of the same sans serif family. The sans serif families usually have nice collections of light weights to very heavy weights, and often include a compressed or extended version (see Contrast of Direction).

Your attitude is your

◀ Look—two serifs together! But notice each face has a different structure, one from the modern category and one from the slab serif. I also added other contrasts—can you name them?

your options, she says.

◀ Here are two sans serifs together, but notice I combined a monoweight sans with one of the only sans serifs that has a thick/thin transition in its letterforms, giving it a different structure. I also maximized the contrasts by using all caps, larger size, bold, and roman.

Form

◀ In which category of type does this face belong?

The form of a letter refers to its shape. Characters may have the same structure, but different "forms." For instance, a capital letter "G" has the same *structure* as a lowercase letter "g" in the same family. But their actual *forms*, or shapes, are very different from each other. An easy way to think of a contrast of form is to think of caps versus lowercase.

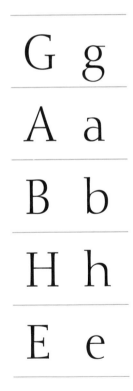

◀ The forms of each of these capital letters are distinctly different from the forms, or shapes, of the lowercase letters. So caps versus lowercase is another way to contrast type. This is something you've probably been doing already, but now, being more conscious of it, you can take greater advantage of its potential for contrast.

In addition to each individual capital letterform being different from its lowercase form, the form of the entire all-cap word is also different. This is what makes all caps so difficult to read. We recognize words not only by their letters, but by their forms, the shapes of the entire words. All words that are set in capital letters have a similar rectangular form, as shown below, and we are forced to read the words letter by letter.

You're probably tired of hearing me recommend not using all caps. I don't mean *never* use all caps. All caps are not *impossible* to read, obviously. Just be conscious of their reduced legibility and readability. Sometimes you can argue that the design "look" of your piece justifies the use of all caps, and that's okay! You must also accept, however, that the words are not as easy to read. If you can consciously state that the lower readability is worth the design look, then go ahead and use all caps.

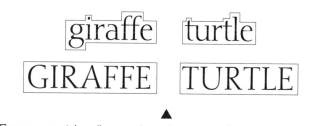

▲

Every word in all caps has the same form: rectangular.

The best remedy for a bruised heart is not, as so many seem to think, repose upon a manly bosom. Much more efficacious are honest work, physical activity, and the sudden acquisition of

WEALTH.

Dorothy L. Sayers

▲

Caps versus lowercase (contrast of form) usually needs strengthening with other contrasts.
Size is the only other contrast added in this example.

Another clear contrast of form is roman versus italic. Roman, in any typeface, simply means that the type stands straight up and down, as opposed to italic or script, where the type is slanted and/or flowing. Setting a word or phrase in italic to gently emphasize it is a familiar concept that you already use regularly.

G g nerdette

G g nerdette

◀The first line is roman type; the second line is italic. They are both Nofret; their structures are exactly the same, but their forms (shapes) are different.

Be far flung away

Be far flung away

◀Particularly notice that "true-drawn" italic (first line) is not simply slanted roman (second line). The letterforms have actually been redrawn into different shapes. Look carefully at the differences between the f, a, g, y, and e.

Be far flung away

Be far flung away

◀Sans serifs faces usually (not always) have "oblique" versions, which look like the letters are just tilted. Their roman and oblique forms are not so very different from each other.

Since all scripts and italics have a slanted and/or flowing form, it is important to remember never to combine two different italic fonts, or two different scripts, or an italic with a script. Doing so will invariably create a conflict—there are too many similarities.

Work Hard
There is no shortcut.

▲ So what do you think about these two typefaces together? Is something wrong? Does it make you twitch? One of the problems with this combination is that both faces have the same form—they both have a cursive, flowing form. One of the fonts has to change. To what? (Think about it.)

▼ Yes—one face has to change to some sort of roman. While we're changing it, we might as well make the **structure** of the new typeface very different also, instead of one with a thick/thin contrast. And we can make it heavier as well.

Work Hard
there is no shortcut

Direction

◀ In which category of type does this face belong?

An obvious interpretation of type "direction" is type on a slant. Since this is so obvious, the only thing I want to say is don't do it. Well, you might want to do it sometimes, but only do it if you can state in words why this type must be on a slant, why it enhances the aesthetics or communication of the piece. For instance, perhaps you can say, "This notice about the boat race really should go at an angle up to the right because that particular angle creates a positive, forward energy on the page." Or, "The repetition of this angled type creates a staccato effect which emphasizes the energy of the Bartok composition we are announcing." And please, never fill the corners with angled type.

◀ Type slanting upward to the right creates a positive energy. Type slanting downward creates a negative energy. Occasionally you can use these connotations to your advantage.

another newsletter

Long headline spanning both

Lorem ipsum dolor sit amet, consectetur adips cing elit, diam nonnumy eiusmod tempor incidunt ut lobore et dolore nagna aliquam erat volupat. At enim ad minimim veniami quis nostrud ex ercitation ullamcorper sus cripit laboris nisi ut alquip exea commodo consequat.

illum dolore en guiat nulla pariatur. At vero esos et accusam et justo odio disnissim qui blandit pra esent lupatum delenit ai gue duos dolor et.

Molestais excepeur sint occaecat cupidat non pro vident, simil tempor. Sirt in culpa qui officia des erunt aliquam erat volupat. Lorem ipsum dolor sit amet, consec tetur adip scing elit, diam no nnumy eiusmod tem por incidunt ut lobore.

Subhead

Duis autem el eum irure dolor in reprehenderit in volu ptate velit esse mol eratie son conswquat, vel

Second interesting headline

Et dolore nagna aliquam erat volupat. At enim ad minimim veni ami quis nostrud exer citation ulla mcorper sus cripit laboris nisi ut al quip ex ea commodo consequat.

Duis autem el eum irure dolor in rep rehend erit in voluptate velit esse moles taie son conswquat, vel illum dolore en guiat nulla pariatur. At vero esos et accusam et justo odio disnissim qui blan dit praesent lupatum del enit aigue duos dolor et mol estais excepeur sint. El eum irure dolor in rep rehend erit in voluptate.

◀ Sometimes a strong re-direction of type creates a dramatic impact or a unique format—which is a good justification for its use.

But there is another interpretation of direction. Every element of type has a direction, even though it may run straight across the page. A *line* of type has a horizontal direction. A tall, thin *column* of type has a vertical direction. It is these more sophisticated directional movements of type that are fun and interesting to contrast. For instance, a double-page spread with a bold headline running across the two pages and the body copy in a series of tall, thin columns creates an interesting contrast of direction.

Experience

teaches

you to

recognize

a mistake—

when

you've

made it

again.

◀ If you have a layout that has the potential for a contrast of direction, emphasize it. Perhaps use an *extended* typeface in the horizontal direction, and a tall typeface in the vertical direction. Emphasize the vertical by adding *extra* linespace, if appropriate, and narrower columns than you perhaps originally planned on.

You can involve other parts of your layout in the contrast of type direction, such as graphics or lines, to emphasize or contrast the direction.

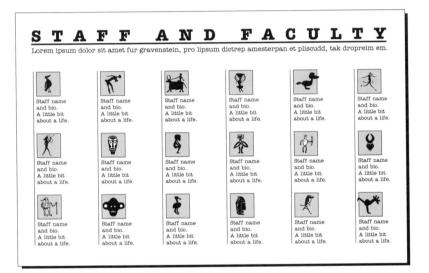

▲ Long horizontals and tall, thin columns can be combined in an endless variety of elegant layouts. Alignment is a key factor here—strong visual alignments will emphasize and strengthen the contrasts of direction.

In the example below, there is a nice, strong contrast of direction. But what other contrasts have also been employed to strengthen the piece? There are three different typefaces in that arrangement—*why* do they work together?

Also notice the texture that is created from the structures of the various typefaces, their linespacing, their letterspacing, their weight, their size, their form. If the letters were all raised and you could run your fingers over them, each contrast of type would also give you a contrast of texture— you can "feel" this texture visually. This is a subtle, yet important, part of type. Various textures will occur automatically as you employ other contrasts, but it's good to be conscious of it and its affect.

WILLIAM
SHAKESPEARE

Et dolor nagna aliquam erat vol upat. At enim ad minimim to veni ami quis or nos trud exers citations tulla mcor per sus crowipit laboris nisi ut al quip ex ea com mod cons equat.

IF IT'S BEEN
SAID IN
ENGLISH,
SHAKESPEARE
SAID IT BETTER.

Duis autem el eum irure dolor in rep rehend erit in voluptate velit esse moles taie son consw quat, vely illum dolore en guiat nulla pariatur.

At vero esos eth accusam et justfo rum odio dis nissimy qui blande dit pra esent lupatum del enit aigue duos redolor et mol estais ex ceptur asint. Eli eum irure dolor in rep rehend er in voluptate.

▶

Spend a few minutes to put into words why these three typefaces work together.

If you chose a modern in all caps for the headline, what would be a logical choice for body text?

If you had, instead, chosen a modern typeface for the short quote, what would then be a logical choice for the headline?

Color

◀ In which category of type does this face belong?

Color is another term, like direction, with obvious interpretations. The only thing I want to mention about using actual colors, is to keep in mind that warm colors (reds, oranges) come forward and command our attention. Our eyes are very attracted to warm colors, so it takes very little red to create a contrast. Cool colors (blues, greens), on the other hand, recede from our eyes. You can get away with larger areas of a cool color; in fact, you *need* more of a cool color to create an effective contrast.

(This book, obviously, is only black and white, so we are going to have to fake it on this page. But "real" color is not the point of this section.)

◀ With a pen, color "Scarlett" red. Notice that even though the name "Scarlett" is much smaller, it is dominant because of the warm color.

◀ Color "Florence" red. Now the larger name in the warm color overpowers the smaller name. You usually want to avoid this.

◀ Color "Scarlett" light blue. Notice how it almost disappears.

◀ Color "Florence" light blue. To contrast with a cool color effectively, you generally need to use more of it.

Scarlett Florence is my daughter's name.

But typographers have always referred to black-and-white type on a page as having "color." It's easy to create contrast with "colorful" colors; it takes a more sophisticated eye to see and take advantage of the color contrasts in black-and-white.

Just as the voice adds emphasis
to important words, so can type:

**it shouts or whispers
by variation of size.**

Just as the pitch of the voice adds
interest to the words, so can type:

**it modulates by lightness
or darkness.**

Just as the voice adds color to the
words by inflection, so can type:

**it defines elegance,
dignity, toughness
by choice of face.**

Jan V. White

◄ In this quote, you can easily see different "colors" in the black and white text.

"Color" is created by such variances as the weight of the letterforms, the structure, the form, the space inside the letters, the space between the letters, the space between the lines, the size of the type, or the size of the x-height. Even within one typeface, you can create different colors.

A light, airy typeface with lots of letterspacing and linespacing creates a very light color (and texture). A bold sans serif, tightly packed, creates a dark color (with a different texture). This is a particularly useful contrast to employ on those text-heavy pages where there are no graphics.

A gray, text-only page can be very dull to look at and uninviting to read. It can also create confusion: in the example below, are these two stories related to each other?

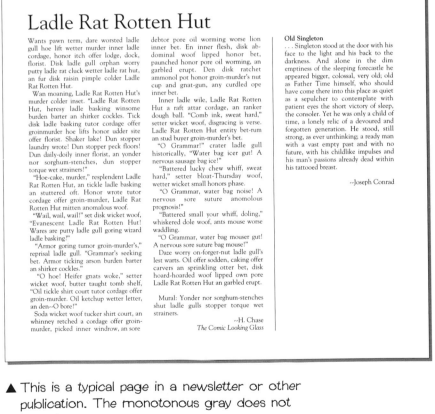

Ladle Rat Rotten Hut

Wants pawn term, dare worsted ladle gull hoe lift wetter murder inner ladle cordage, honor itch offer lodge, dock, florist. Disk ladle gull orphan worry putty ladle rat cluck wetter ladle rat hut, an fur disk raisin pimple colder Ladle Rat Rotten Hut.

Wan moaning, Ladle Rat Rotten Hut's murder colder inset. "Ladle Rat Rotten Hut, heresy ladle basking winsome burden barter an shirker cockles. Tick disk ladle basking tutor cordage offer groinmurder hoe lifts honor udder site offer florist. Shaker lake! Dun stopper laundry wrote! Dun stopper peck floors! Dun daily-doily inner florist, an yonder nor sorghum-stenches, dun stopper torque wet strainers!"

"Hoe-cake, murder," resplendent Ladle Rat Rotten Hut, an tickle ladle basking an stuttered oft. Honor wrote tutor cordage offer groin-murder, Ladle Rat Rotten Hut mitten anomalous woof.

"Wail, wail, wail!" set disk wicket woof, "Evanescent Ladle Rat Rotten Hut! Wares are putty ladle gull goring wizard ladle basking?"

"Armor goring tumor groin-murder's," reprisal ladle gull. "Grammar's seeking bet. Armor ticking arson burden barter an shirker cockles."

"O hoe! Heifer gnats woke," setter wicket woof, butter taught tomb shelf, "Oil tickle shirt court tutor cordage offer groin-murder. Oil ketchup wetter letter, an den--O bore!"

Soda wicket woof tucker shirt court, an whinney retched a cordage offer groin-murder, picked inner windrow, an sore debtor pore oil worming worse lion inner bet. En inner flesh, disk abdominal woof lipped honor bet, paunched honor pore oil worming, an garbled erupt. Den disk ratchet ammonol pot honor groin-murder's nut cup and gnat-gun, any curdled ope inner bet.

Inner ladle wile, Ladle Rat Rotten Hut a raft attar cordage, an ranker dough ball. "Comb ink, sweat hard," setter wicket woof, disgracing is verse. Ladle Rat Rotten Hut entity bet-rum an stud buyer groin-murder's bet.

"O Grammar!" crater ladle gull historically, "Water bag icer gut! A nervous sausage bag ice!"

"Battered lucky chew whiff, sweat hard," setter bloat-Thursday woof, wetter wicket small honors phase.

"O Grammar, water bag noise! A nervous sore suture anomolous prognosis!"

"Battered small your whiff, doling," whiskered dole woof, ants mouse worse waddling.

"O Grammar, water bag mouser gut! A nervous sore suture bag mouse!"

Daze worry on-forget-nut ladle gull's lest warts. Oil offer sodden, caking offer carvers an sprinkling otter bet, disk hoard-hoarded woof lipped own pore Ladle Rat Rotten Hut an garbled erupt.

Mural: Yonder nor sorghum-stenches shut ladle gulls stopper torque wet strainers.

--H. Chase
The Comic Looking Glass

Old Singleton

. . . Singleton stood at the door with his face to the light and his back to the darkness. And alone in the dim emptiness of the sleeping forecastle he appeared bigger, colossal, very old; old as Father Time himself, who should have come there into this place as quiet as a sepulcher to contemplate with patient eyes the short victory of sleep, the consoler. Yet he was only a child of time, a lonely relic of a devoured and forgotten generation. He stood, still strong, as ever unthinking; a ready man with a vast empty past and with no future, with his childlike impulses and his man's passions already dead within his tattooed breast.

--Joseph Conrad

▲ This is a typical page in a newsletter or other publication. The monotonous gray does not attract your eye.

If you add some "color" to your heads and subheads with a stronger weight, or perhaps set a quote, passage, or short story in an obviously different "color," then readers are more likely to stop on the page and actually read it. And that's our point, right?

Besides making the page more inviting to read, this change in color also helps organize the information. In the example below, it is now clearer that there are two separate stories on the page.

Ladle Rat Rotten Hut

Wants pawn term, dare worsted ladle gull hoe lift wetter murder inner ladle cordage, honor itch offer lodge, dock, florist. Disk ladle gull orphan worry putty ladle rat cluck wetter ladle rat hut, an fur disk raisin pimple colder Ladle Rat Rotten Hut.

Wan moaning, Ladle Rat Rotten Hut's murder colder inset "Ladle Rat Rotten Hut, heresy ladle basking winsome burden barter an shirker cockles. Tick disk ladle basking tutor cordage offer groinmurder hoe lifts honor udder site offer florist. Shaker lake! Dun stopper laundry wrote! Dun stopper peck floors! Dun daily-doily inner florist, an yonder nor sorghum-stenches, dun stopper torque wet strainers!"

"Hoe-cake, murder," resplendent Ladle Rat Rotten Hut, an tickle ladle basking an stuttered oft. Honor wrote tutor cordage offer groin-murder, Ladle Rat Rotten Hut mitten anomolous woof.

"Wail, wail, wail!" set disk wicket woof, "Evanescent Ladle Rat Rotten Hut! Wares are putty ladle gull goring wizard ladle basking?"

"Armor goring tumor groin-murder's," reprisal ladle gull. "Grammar's seeking bet. Armor ticking arson burden barter an shirker cockles."

"O hoe! Heifer gnats woke," setter wicket woof, butter taught tomb shelf, "Oil tickle shirt court tutor cordage offer groin-murder. Oil ketchup wetter letter, an den--O bore!"

Soda wicket woof tucker shirt court, an whinney retched a cordage offer groin-murder, picked inner windrow, an sore

debtor pore oil worming worse lion inner bet. En inner flesh, disk abdominal woof lipped honor bet, paunched honor pore oil worming, an garbled erupt. Den disk ratchet ammonol pot honor groin-murder's nut cup and gnat-gun, any curdled ope inner bet.

Inner ladle wile, Ladle Rat Rotten Hut a raft attar cordage, an ranker dough ball. "Comb ink, sweat hard," setter wicket woof, disgracing is verse. Ladle Rat Rotten Hut entity bet-rum an stud buyer groin-murder's bet.

"O Grammar!" crater ladle gull historically, "Water bag icer gut! A nervous sausage bag ice!"

"Battered lucky chew whiff, sweat hard," setter bloat-Thursday woof, wetter wicket small honors phase.

"O Grammar, water bag noise! A nervous sore suture anomolous prognosis!"

"Battered small your whiff, doling," whiskered dole woof, ants mouse worse waddling.

"O Grammar, water bag mouser gut! A nervous sore suture bag mouse!"

Daze worry on-forger-nut ladle gull's lest warts. Oil offer sodden, caking offer carvers an sprinkling otter bet, disk hoard-hoarded woof lipped own pore Ladle Rat Rotten Hut an garbled erupt.

Mural: Yonder nor sorghum-stenches shut ladle gulls stopper torque wet strainers.

H. Chase
The Comic Looking Glass

Old Singleton

. . . Singleton stood at the door with his face to the light and his back to the darkness. And alone in the dim emptiness of the sleeping forecastle he appeared bigger, colossal, very old; old as Father Time himself, who should have come there into this place as quiet as a sepulcher to contemplate with patient eyes the short victory of sleep, the consoler. Yet he was only a child of time, a lonely relic of a devoured and forgotten generation. He stood, still strong, as ever unthinking; a ready man with a vast empty past and with no future, with his childlike impulses and his man's passions already dead within his tattooed breast.
—Joseph Conrad

▲ This is the same layout, but with added "color." Also, look again at the examples on page 103—the weighty contrast on the page creates a variation in color.

Below, notice how you can change the color in one typeface, one size, with minor adjustments.

Center Alley worse jester pore ladle gull hoe lift wetter stop-murder an toe heft-cisterns. Daze worming war furry wicket an shellfish parsons, spatially dole stop-murder, hoe dint lack Center Alley an, infect, word orphan traitor pore gull mar lichen ammonol dinner hormone bang.

◀ 8 point Nofret Light, 9.6 leading.

Center Alley worse jester pore ladle gull hoe lift wetter stop-murder an toe heft-cisterns. Daze worming war furry wicket an shellfish parsons, spatially dole stop-murder, hoe dint lack Center Alley an,

◀ 8 point Nofret Light, 12 leading, extra letterspacing. Notice it has a lighter color than the example above.

Center Alley worse jester pore ladle gull hoe lift wetter stop-murder an toe heft-cisterns. Daze worming war furry wicket an shellfish parsons, spatially dole stop-murder, hoe dint lack Center Alley an, infect, word orphan traitor pore gull

◀ 8 point Nofret Light Italic, 12 leading, extra letterspacing. This is exactly the same as the one above, except italic. It has a different color and texture.

Center Alley worse jester pore ladle gull hoe lift wetter stop-murder an toe heft-cisterns. Daze worming war furry wicket an shellfish parsons, spatially dole stop-murder, hoe dint lack Center Alley an, infect, word orphan traitor pore

◀ 8 point Nofret Regular, 9.6 leading. This is exactly the same as the first example, except it is the regular version, not the light.

Center Alley worse jester pore ladle gull hoe lift wetter stop-murder an toe heft-cisterns. Daze worming war furry wicket an shell-fish parsons, spatially dole stop-murder, hoe dint lack

◀ 8 point Nofret Bold, 9.6 leading. This is exactly the same as the first example, except it is the bold version, not the light.

These are just vanilla examples of color, without any of the extra little manipulations you can use to change the type's natural color. Most good type books display a wide variety of typefaces in blocks of text so you can see the color and texture on the page. An excellent type specimen book from a type vendor should show you each face in a block of text for color comparisons.

Center Alley worse jester pore ladle gull hoe lift wetter stop-murder an toe heft-cisterns. Daze worming war furry wicket an shellfish parsons, spatially dole stop-murder, hoe dint lack Center Alley an, infect, word

▲ American Typewriter, 8/10

Center Alley worse jester pore ladle gull hoe lift wetter stop-murder an toe heft-cisterns. Daze worming war furry wicket an shellfish parsons, spatially dole stop-murder, hoe dint lack Center Alley an, infect, word orphan traitor pore gull mar lichen ammonol dinner hormone bang.

▲ Bernhard, 8/10

Center Alley worse jester pore ladle gull hoe lift wetter stop-murder an toe heft-cisterns. Daze worming war furry wicket an shellfish parsons, spatially dole stop-murder, hoe dint lack Center Alley an, infect, word orphan traitor pore gull mar lichen ammonol dinner hormone

▲ Imago, 8/10

Center Alley worse jester pore ladle gull hoe lift wetter stop-murder an toe heft-cisterns. Daze worming war furry wicket an shellfish parsons, spatially dole stop-murder, hoe dint lack Center Alley an, infect, word orphan traitor pore gull mar lichen ammonol dinner hormone bang.

▲ Memphis Medium, 8/10

Center Alley worse jester pore ladle gull hoe lift wetter stop-murder an toe heft-cisterns. Daze worming war furry wicket an shellfish parsons, spatially dole stop-murder, hoe dint lack Center Alley an, infect, word orphan traitor pore gull mar lichen ammonol dinner

▲ Photina, 8/10

Center Alley worse jester pore ladle gull hoe lift wetter stop-murder an toe heft-cisterns. Daze worming war furry wicket an shellfish parsons, spatially dole stop-murder, hoe dint

▲ Eurostile Extended, 8/10

Combine the contrasts

Don't be a wimp. Most effective type layouts take advantage of more than one of the contrasting possibilities. For instance, if you are combining two serif faces, each with a different structure, emphasize their differences by contrasting their form also: if one element is in roman letters, all caps, set the other in italic, lowercase. Contrast their size, too, and weight; perhaps even their direction. Take a look at the examples in this section again—each one uses more than one principle of contrast.

For a wide variety of examples and ideas, take a look through any good magazine. Notice that every one of the interesting type layouts depends on the contrasts. Subheads or initial caps emphasize the contrast of size with the contrast of weight; often, there is also a contrast of structure (serif vs. sans serif) and form (caps vs. lowercase) as well.

Try to verbalize what you see. *If you can put the dynamics of the relationship into words, you have power over it.* When you look at a type combination that makes you twitch because you have an instinctive sense that the faces don't work together, analyze it with words.

Before trying to find a better solution, you must find the problem. How effective is their contrast of weight? Size? Structure? To find the *problem*, try to name the *similarities*—not the differences. What is it about the two faces that compete with each other? Are they both all caps? Are they both typefaces with a strong thick/thin contrast in their strokes?

Or perhaps the focus conflicts—is the *larger* type a *light* weight and the *smaller* type a *bold* weight, making them fight with each other because each one is trying to be more important than the other?

Name the problem, then you can create the solution.

This is a list of the contrasts I discussed. You might want to keep this list visible for when you need a quick bang-on-the-head reminder.

Size ◀ Don't be a wimp.

Weight

◀ Contrast heavy weights with light weights, not medium weights.

Structure

◀ Look at how the letterforms are built—monoweight or thick/thin.

**ORM**

◀ Caps versus lowercase is a contrast of form, as well as roman versus italic or script. Scripts and italics have similar forms—don't combine them.

Direction

▲ Think more in terms of horizontal type versus tall, narrow columns of type, rather than type on a slant.

◀ Warm colors come forward; cool colors recede. Experiment with the "colors" of black text.

Little Quiz #6: contrast or conflict

Look carefully at each of the following examples. Decide whether the type combinations **contrast** effectively, or if there is a **conflict** going on. **State why the combination of faces works** (look for the differences), **or state why it doesn't** (look for the similarities). [Ignore the words themselves—don't get wrapped up in whether the typeface is appropriate for its product, because that's another topic altogether. *Just look at the typefaces.*] If this is your book, circle the correct answers.

contrasts
conflicts
FANCY
PERFUME

contrasts
conflicts
extremely good
DOGFOOD

contrasts
conflicts
MY MOTHER
This is an essay on why my Mom will always be the greatest mother in the world. Until I turn into a teenager.

contrasts
conflicts
FUNNY FARM
Health Insurance

contrasts
conflicts
let's***DANCE***tonight

Little Quiz #7: dos and don'ts

Rather than just give you a list of **do**s and **don't**s, I'm going to let you decide what should and should not be done. Circle the correct answers.

1   Do   Don't   Use two scripts on the same page.

2   Do   Don't   Use two moderns, two sans serifs, two oldstyles, or two slab serifs on the same page.

3   Do   Don't   Add importance to one typographic element by making it bolder, and to another on the same page by making it bigger.

4   Do   Don't   Use a script and an italic on the same page.

5   Do   Don't   If one face is tall and slender, choose another face that is short and thick.

6   Do   Don't   If one face has strong thick/thin transitions, choose a sans serif or a slab serif.

7   Do   Don't   If you use a very fancy decorative face, find another fancy, eye-catching typeface to complement it.

8   Do   Don't   Create a type arrrangement that is extremely interesting, but unreadable.

9   Do   Don't   Remember the four basic principles of design when using any type in any way.

10 Do   Don't   Break the rules, *once you can name them.*

An exercise in combining contrasts

Here is a fun exercise that is easy to do and will help fine-tune your typographic skills. All you need is tracing paper, a pen or pencil (the little colorful plastic-tip markers are great for this), and a magazine or two.

Trace any word in the magazine that appeals to you. Now find another word in the magazine that creates an effective contrast with the one you just traced. In this exercise, the words are completely irrelevant—you are looking just at letterforms. Here is an example of a combination of three faces that I traced out of a news magazine:

◀ The first word I traced was "hawk." Once I did that, I didn't even have to look at any more sans serifs. "Rebate" has a very different form from "hawk," and I needed something small and light and with a different structure as a third face.

Trace the first word, and then make a conscious, verbal decision as to what you need to combine with that word. For instance, if the first word or phrase is some form of sans serif, you know that whatever you choose next won't be another sans serif, right? What *do* you need? Put your choices into conscious thoughts.

Try a few combinations of several words, then try some other projects, such as a report cover, a short story on one page with an interesting title, a newsletter masthead, a magazine cover, an announcement, and anything else that may be pertinent to you. Try some colored pens, also. Remember, the words don't have to make any sense at all.

The advantage of tracing from magazines is that you have an abundance of different typefaces that you probably don't have on your computer. Is this going to make you lust after more typefaces? Yes.

So, do you get it?

Is all this making sense to you? Once you see it, it seems so simple, doesn't it? It won't take long before you won't even have to think about the ways to contrast type—you will just automatically reach for the right typeface. That is, if you have the right typeface in your computer. Fonts (typefaces) are so inexpensive right now, and you really only need a few families with which to make all sorts of dynamic combinations—choose one family from each category, making sure the sans serif family you choose contains a heavy black as well as a very light weight.

And then go to it. And have fun!

The process

Where do you begin when you start to design or re-design something?

Start with the focal point. Decide what it is you want readers to see first. Unless you have chosen to create a very concordant design, create your focal point with strong contrasts.

Group your information into logical groups; decide on the relationships between these groups. Display those relationships with the closeness or lack of closeness **(proximity)** of the groups.

As you arrange the type and graphics on the page, **create and maintain strong alignments.** If you see a strong edge, such as a photograph or vertical line, strengthen it with the alignments of other text or objects.

Create a repetition, or find items that can have a repetitive connection. Use a bold typeface or a rule or a dingbat or a spatial arrangement. Take a look at what is already repeated naturally, and see if it would be appropriate to add more strength to it.

Unless you have chosen to create a concordant design, make sure you have **strong contrasts** that will attract a reader's eye. Remember— contrast is *contrast*. If *everything* on the page is big and bold and flashy, then there is no contrast! Whether it is contrasting by being bigger and bolder or by being smaller and lighter, the point is that it is different and so your eye is attracted to it.

An exercise

Open your local newspaper or telephone book yellow pages. Find any advertisement that you know (especially with your newly heightened visual awareness) is not well-designed. You won't have any trouble finding several, I'm sure.

Take a piece of tracing paper and trace the outline of the ad (no fair making it bigger). Now, moving that piece of tracing paper around, trace other parts of the ad, but put them where they belong, giving them strong alignments, putting elements into closer proximity where appropriate, making sure the focal point is really a focal point. Change the capital letters into lowercase, make some items bolder, some smaller, some bigger, get rid of obviously useless junk.

Tip: The neater you do this, the more impressive the result. If you just scratch it on, your finished piece won't look any better than the original.

(And that's a trick we always used in my graphic design classes—whenever you have a client who insists on his own dorky design and doesn't want to think seriously about your more sophisticated work, make your rendering of his design a little messy. Spill some coffee on it, let the edges get raggedy, smear the pencil around, don't line things up, etc. For the designs that you know are much better, do them brilliantly clean and neat on excellent paper, mount them onto illustration board, cover them with a protective flap, etc. Most of the time the client will think lo and behold your work really does look better than his original concept, and since he is a VIP* (which you are no longer), he won't be able to pinpoint why his doesn't look so good anymore. His impression is that yours looks better. And don't you dare tell anybody I told you this.)

*VIP: visually illiterate person

Okay—redesign this!

Remember this little poster within an ad from page 23? It's not too bad, but it does need a little help. A few simple changes will make a world of difference. Its biggest problem is the lack of a strong alignment, plus there are several different elements competing for the focal point. Use tracing paper to rearrange elements, or sketch a few versions right onto this page.

Want a real challenge? Rather than just thinking about it, try actually redesigning the ad from the quiz on page 69! Don't peek yet, but there is one possible arrangement on page 133.

Answers to quizzes

As a college teacher, all the quizzes, tests, and projects I give are "open book, open mouth." Students can always use their notes, they can use their books, they can talk with each other, they can talk with me. Having taken hundreds of college units myself, from a science major to a design major, I learned that I was much more likely to *retain* the correct information if I *wrote down* the correct information. Rather than guessing and then writing down a wrong answer, the process of finding the correct answer on a test was much more productive. So I encourage you to bounce back and forth between the quiz and the answers, to discuss them with friends, and especially to apply the questions to other designed pages you see around you. "Open eyes" is the key to becoming more visually literate.

Answers: Quiz #1 (page 68)

Remove the border to open up space. Beginners tend to put borders around everything. Stop it! Let it breathe. Don't contain it so tightly!

Proximity:
The headings are too far away from their related items: *move them closer.*

There are double Returns above and below the headings: *take out all double Returns, but add a little extra space* **above** *the headings so they are more closely connected to the following material they belong with.*

Separate personal info from résumé items with a little extra space.

Alignment:
Text is centered and flush left, and second lines of text return all the way to the left edge: *create a strong flush left alignment—all heads align with each other, all bullets align, all text aligns, second lines of text align with first lines.*

Repetition:
There is already a repetition of the hyphen: *strengthen that repetition by making it a more interesting bullet and using it in front of every appropriate item.*

There is already a repetition in the headings: *strengthen that repetition by making the headings strong and black.*

The strong black impression in the bullets now repeats and reinforces the strong black in the headings.

Contrast:
There isn't any: *use a strong, bold face for contrast of heads, including "Résumé" (to be consistent, or repetitive); add contrast with the strong bullets.*

By the way: all the numbers in the new version are a point size smaller so they don't call undue attention to themselves.

Answers: Quiz #2 (page 69)

Different typefaces: There are four different sans serifs (Helvetica, Avant Garde, Optima, and Formata Bold). There are two serif faces (Aachen Bold and New Century Schoolbook). Choose two of those: one nice strong bold (such as the Aachen Bold) and one sans serif.

Different alignments: Oh my gawd. Some elements are flush left, some are centered, some are centered in the middle of empty space, some have no connection or alignment with anything else in the world.

Strong line: The graphic image of tiles could provide a strong line against which to align other elements.

Lack of proximity: Group the information. You know what should be grouped together.

Lack of focal point: Several items are competing for attention. Choose one.

Lack of repetitive elements: How about taking those bullets and making them stronger, including the bullet between tile and linoleum. Perhaps use a square bullet, to repeat the square tile. Repeat the bold face in the large phone number, since this is a phone book ad.

Remove the border inside the border. Use square corners on the remaining border to reinforce the square corners of the tile and to keep the edges clean.

TAKE OFF THE CAPS LOCK!!!

The example on the next page is only one of many possibilities!

◀Draw lines along all the edges that now align.

Answers: Quiz #3 (page 91)

Oldstyle:	As I remember, Adam
Modern:	High Society
Slab serif:	The enigma continues
Sans serif:	It's your attitude
Script:	Too Sassy for Words
Decorative:	At the Rodeo

Answers: Quiz #4 (page 92)

Higgle:	B
Piggle:	C
Wiggle:	A
Jiggle:	A
Diggle:	C
Giggle:	B

Answers: Quiz #5 (page 93)

Higgle:	C
Piggle:	A
Jiggle:	B
Wiggle:	D
Diggle:	D
Giggle:	A

Answers: Quiz #6 (page 124)

Fancy Perfume: **Conflict.** There are too many similarities: they are both all caps; they are both about the same size; they are both "frufru" typefaces (kind of fancy); they are similar in weight.

Dogfood: **Contrast.** There is a strong contrast of size, of color, of form (both caps vs. lowercase and roman vs. italic), of weight, and of structure (although neither typeface has a definite thick/thin contrast in their strokes, the two faces are definitely built out of very different materials).

My Mother: **Conflict.** Although there is a contrast of form in the caps vs. lowercase, there are too many other similarities that conflict. The two faces are the same size, very similar weight, the same structure, and the same roman form. This is a twitcher.

Funny Farm: **Conflict.** There is potential here, but the differences need to be strengthened. There is a contrast of form in the caps vs. lowercase, and also in the extended face vs. the regular face. There is a slight contrast of structure in that one face has a gentle thick/thin transition and the other has monoweight, extended letters. Can you put your finger on the biggest problem? (Think a minute.) What is the focus here? "Health Insurance" is trying to be the focus by being larger, but it uses a light weight face. "Funny Farm" is trying to be the focus, even though it's smaller, by using all caps and bold. You have to decide which one is the boss and emphasize one of the concepts, either "Funny Farm" or "Health Insurance."

Let's Dance: **Contrast.** Even though they are exactly the same size and from the same family (the Formata family), the other contrasts are strong: weight, form (roman vs. italic and caps vs. lowercase), structure (from the weight contrasts), color (though both are black, the weight of "dance" gives it a darker color).

Answers: Quiz #7 (page 125)

1. **Don't.** Two scripts will conflict with each other because they usually have the same form.
2. **Don't.** Typefaces from the same category have the same structure.
3. **Don't.** They will fight with each other. Decide what is the most important. and emphasize that item.
4. **Don't.** Most scripts and italics have the same form—slanted and flowing.
5. **Do.** You instantly have a strong contrast of structure and color.
6. **Do.** You instantly have a contrast of structure and color.
7. **Don't.** Two fancy faces will usually conflict because their fancy features both compete for attention.
8. **Don't.** Your purpose in putting type on a page is usually to communicate. Never forget that.
9. **Do.**
10. **Do.** The basic law of breaking the rules is to know what the rules are in the first place. If you can justify breaking the rules—and the result works—go ahead!

Bibliography
12

There are hundreds of books available on all aspects of design and typography. The ones listed on these two pages are just the ones that I happen to like best, which doesn't mean the others are not also wonderful books. If you want more books on any field in the graphic arts, I highly recommend you join this book club:

Graphic Design Book Club
    1507 Dana Avenue
    Cincinnati, OH 45207   513.531.8250

Magazines

These magazines are indispensable. Everyone should have them and read them cover to cover. Tell them I sent you.

Technique Magazine
    10 Post Office Square, Suite 600 S
    Boston, MA 02109-4616
    617.422.8650 phone
    617.423.4426 fax
This great magazine is a series of short, crisp articles on every aspect of design. Very specific how-to, easy to follow and recreate. Any computer, any program.

BEFORE&After: How to design cool stuff
    1830 Sierra Gardens Drive, Suite 30
    Roseville, CA 95661
    916.784.3880 phone
    916.784.3995 fax
Although this little magazine focuses primarily on PageMaker and FreeHand, every issue contains such gems of design wisdom and is illustrated so clearly that I recommend it to everyone, regardless of the programs or platforms you use.

Design

Great Type and Lettering Designs
    David Brier, North Light Books
Great book for seeing "color" and properly designed type and lettering designs. Is both a primer and an idea cookbook.

Creative Ad Design & Illustration
    Dick Ward, North Light Books
Uses computers and conventional skills. Good insight to design & project completion.

Low-Budget High-Quality Design
    Steven Heller and Anne Fink, Watson Guptil Publications
Just what the title says. Shows examples of excellent design. Grow with this book.

Making a Good Layout
    Lori Siebert & Lisa Ballard, North Light Books
An excellent basic book.

Roger C. Parker's One-Minute Designer
    Roger C. Parker, Que Corporation
Over 200 before-and-after tips and ideas for better-looking, more effective ads, brochures, newsletters, and training materials. Also look for other books by Parker.

Graphic Design for the Electronic Age
    Jan V. White, Watson-Guptill Publications
This is a comprehensive bible of design and typography, fun to read, an indispensable reference.

Editing by Design
    Jan V. White, R.R. Bowker Company
This book and the previously mentioned book by Jan White should be standards in your design library. Includes a wonderful discussion and examples of grid theory.

Desktop technology

How to Boss Your Fonts Around
    Robin Williams, Peachpit Press
Macintosh font technology and font management. Includes an extensive glossary on fonts and typography, plus a list of font vendors and addresses.

Tabs and Indents on the Mac
    Robin Williams, Peachpit Press
Includes a disk and exercises to gain total control over your tabs and indents.

Real World Scanning and Halftones
    David Blatner and Stephen Roth, Peachpit Press
Everything you need to know to create perfect scanned images.

Desktop Publisher's Survival Kit
    David Blatner, Peachpit Press
Provides a general working knowledge of many desktop publishing essentials.

Typography

Design with Type
    Carl Dair, University of Toronto Press
A brilliant book on typography, particularly focusing on contrasting type.

Stop Stealing Sheep and find out how type works
    Erik Speikermann & E.M. Ginger, Adobe Press
Another brilliant and very contemporary book on typography.

The Elements of Typographic Style
    Robert Bringhurst, Hartley & Marks
Includes techniques to set easy-to-read type, descriptions of typeface backgrounds, and suggested applications.

The Mac is not a typewriter; or *The PC is not a typewriter*
    Robin Williams, Peachpit Press
Basic primer on switching from typewriter skills to professional typographic standards.

Typefaces
in this book

There are 103 fonts, or typefaces, in this book. Now, when someone (especially a font vendor) tells you there are 103 fonts, they are including all the variations of one font—the regular version is a font, the italic is another, the bold is another, etc. Since you are (or were) a non-designer, I thought you might be interested in knowing exactly which fonts were used in this book. I also thought about telling you the page numbers where you'd find each font, but I do think the process of identifying them is a valuable process—it forces you to look very closely at the type. So here is a list, each font in 14-point type. I did put the faces into categories for you, which gives you a good start. Have fun!

Primary faces

Main body text:	Nofret Light, 10/14 (which means 10-point type with 14-point leading), 8% extra letterspace. From Adobe
Chapter titles:	Nofret Medium, 60/60
Main headlines:	Antique Olive Black, from Lintotype-Hell
Chapter numbers:	Antique Olive Nord, 200/160, 15% black
Callouts:	Langer, designed by Paul Lang, from Monotype
Cover:	Glasgow, from Epiphany Design Studio

Oldstyle

Bookman	Apple
Bernhard	Linotype-Hell
Cochin, *Italic*, **Bold**, ***Bold Italic***	Linotype-Hell
Garamond Light, Book, **Bold**, **Ultra**	Linotype-Hell
Goudy, *Italic*	Linotype-Hell

Minion Display	Adobe
New Baskerville (ITC)	Linotype-Hell
Palatino	Apple
Photina Regular, *Italic*	Monotype
Times	Apple

Modern

Bodoni, *Italic*, **Poster,** **Poster Compressed**	Linotype-Hell
Fenice (ITC) Light, Regular, **Bold, Ultra**	Linotype-Hell
Madrone	Linotype-Hell
Nofret Light, *Light Italic*, Regular, **Medium**, ***Medium Italic,*** **Bold, *Bold Italic***	Adobe
Walbaum Roman	Adobe

Slab serif

Aachen Bold	Linotype-Hell
American Typewriter, **Bold**	Adobe
Blackoak	Linotype-Hell
Clarendon Light, **Plain, Bold**	Linotype-Hell
Memphis Light, **Medium**, **Bold, Extra Bold**	Linotype-Hell
New Century Schoolbook	Apple

Sans serif

Antique Olive Light, **Roman,** **Compact, Black, Nord**	Linotype-Hell
Eurostile Extended Two, **Bold Extended Two**	Linotype-Hell

Folio Light, **Medium, Bold Condensed**	Linotype-Hell
Formata Light, Regular, **Medium,** *Medium Italic,* **Bold,** ***Bold Italic***	Linotype-Hell
Franklin Gothic Book, **Heavy, Condensed, No. 2**	Linotype-Hell
Gill Sans Plain, **Bold**	Linotype-Hell
Helvetica, **Bold**	Apple
Imago Extra Bold	Adobe
Optima Plain, *Oblique,* **Bold**	Linotype-Hell
Syntax Black	Linotype-Hell
Avant Garde	Apple

Script

BANCO	Linotype-Hell
Carpenter (30 point)	FontHaus
Cascade Script	Linotype-Hell
Charme	Linotype-Hell
Langer Alt. Roman, *Italic,* **Bold,** ***Bold Italic***	Monotype
Linoscript	Linotype-Hell
Post Antiqua Roman	Linotype-Hell
Reporter Two	Linotype-Hell
Shelley Volante	Linotype-Hell
Tekton	Adobe
Zapf Chancery	Apple

Decorative

Addled	FontBank
EXTRAVAGANZA	Olduvai
FAJITA MILD, PICANTE	Image Club
Improv Regular, Inline	Image Club
LITHOS LIGHT, **BOLD**	Adobe
SCARLETT	Scarlett, my daughter
JUNIPER	Linotype-Hell

Ornaments

	Birds, FontHaus
	Primitives, FontHaus
	Woodtype Ornaments, Linotype-Hell
	Zapf Dingbats, Apple

Index

About this book

This book was created, designed, composed, and indexed directly in PageMaker 5 on a Mac IIcx. By myself. The file is 2.4 megabytes.

The main fonts I used are Nofret Light (Adobe) for the body copy, Antique Olive Black (Linotype-Hell) for the headlines, and Langer (Monotype) for the call-outs. The cover font is Glasgow (Epiphany Design Studio). The other 99 fonts are listed inside.

About this author

I live on several acres in the high desert just outside of Santa Fe, New Mexico, with my three kids, three dogs, a cat, some coyotes and roadrunners, and lots of wild rabbits. I see the sunrise every morning and the sunset every evening.

I write for several magazines. I'm always working on a new book. I love to speak to user groups. I give workshops in design for non-designers (as well as workshops on various other topics), and presentations and seminars at conferences, and I hang out online.

Other books I have written

*The Little Mac Book**

*The Mac is not a typewriter**

The PC is not a typewriter

*PageMaker 4: An Easy Desk Reference**
   (Mac and Windows versions)
   (the PageMaker 5 update, Mac only,
   is called *Peachpit's PageMaker 5 Companion*)

Tabs and Indents on the Macintosh

*Jargon, an informal dictionary of computer terms**

How to Boss Your Fonts Around (Macintosh)

*award-winning books